Flowing with the River

For Marg,
Happy Reading!
Sue Dec. 20/13

Flowing with the River

Soundings from my Life and Ministry

Sue Clemmer Steiner

Photos by Samuel J. Steiner

Flowing with the River
Copyright © 2013 Sue Clemmer Steiner
All rights reserved.

Steiner, Susan Clemmer, 1947-, author
    Flowing with the river : soundings from my life and ministry / Sue Clemmer Steiner ; Samuel J. Steiner (photos).

ISBN 978-0-9811516-2-5 (pbk.)

    1. Steiner, Susan Clemmer, 1947-. 2. Mennonites--Clergy--Biography. I. Steiner, Samuel J., photographer II. Title.

BX8143.S74A3 2013   289.7092   C2013-905304-2

Unless otherwise noted, Scripture text is quoted from New Revised Standard Version Bible, copyright 1989, Division of Christian Education of the National Council of the Churches of Christ in the United States of America. Used by permission. All rights reserved.

"i thank You God for most this amazing". Copyright 1950, © 1978, 1991 by the Trustees for the E.E. Cummings Trust. Copyright © 1979 by George James Firmage, from COMPLETE POEMS: 1904-1962 by E.E. Cummings, edited by George J. Firmage. Used by permission of Liveright Publishing Corporation.

Cover and book design by Christian Snyder.

Self-published in Canada. Printed at Pandora Print Shop.

Copies available from Sue C. Steiner (scsteiner@sympatico.ca)

For Sam
Beloved Life Companion
44 years and counting

Then the angel showed me the river of the water of life, bright as crystal, flowing from the throne of God and of the Lamb through the middle of the street of the city. On either side of the river is the tree of life with its twelve kinds of fruit, producing its fruit each month; and the leaves of the tree are for the healing of the nations. Revelation 22: 1-2 NRSV

My desire
is to be in the stream of history
moving ever more fully towards God
…basking in God's steady, sturdy love towards me
…moving with the current as it flows
…knowing where some deeper currents lie
and inviting others in.

My nothing distract me from flowing with this stream.

Table of Contents

Foreword by Brice Balmer — 9
Author's Preface: Sharing the River Journey — 11

Getting Oriented
Pounding Surf, Many Shorelines — 15
Claimed by the Conestogo — 21

Nourished on the River Banks
Between Stink Creek and the River of Life — 29
Feasting by the River: Mom's Company Tables — 37
Gentle Breezes off the River: Three Vignettes — 43

Testing the Waters
Navigating Churning Waters: *The Goshen College Record* — 51
Plunged into the River: i thank You God — 57
Immersed in Story — 61
A Bracing Wind: Miller Time — 67
A Tsunami of Tears — 71

Finding a Ministry Flow
From Showy Lady Slippers to Varied Fen Flowers — 77
Life on the River Flats: Staying Connected to the Vine — 83
Paddling Furiously: Beyond Hard Work — 89
At Rest: Colpoys Bay — 97

Fed by Underground Streams

The Clemmer Farm	103
Maggie Uncovered	107

Exploring the Watershed

The Susquehanna: Discovering a Vast Watershed	117
Rituals on the River: Then and Now	123
Dancing Chalice	131
Preaching: An Intimate Act	135
Baptism Sermon: You Are God's Beloved	141
Reflection: The Ohio at Ripley	145
Surprised by God's Spirit: Rowing across the Current	147

Navigating Uncharted Waters

Roaring Waters: Grief, Longing and Delicate New Life	157
The River Journey Continues	163
Afterword: Meditation by a Kentucky Pond	169

Gratitudes	171
About the Author	173

Foreword

While Sue Steiner reflects on her journey into and through her ministry, I have remembered my own call and the experiences and people who were critical on my path. This memoir is not only written for us to learn more about one woman's voyage, though the struggles of the first and second generation of women in ministry in the Mennonite church are very present here. This is also a spiritual autobiography through which we can see ourselves and our own call "to follow Christ in life."

For the past 30 years, Sue and I have compared notes as we both have been ministers in Mennonite Church Eastern Canada. How do our personalities and experiences earlier in life influence how we live out our callings? How do we provide leadership in times of great change in our society? How are we growing spiritually as we care for others?

Sue and I have also co-taught the final course in the Master of Theological Studies (ministry stream) at Conrad Grebel University College, where we examined models of leadership and the grounding for ministry. I value this book as another resource for training leaders for whom examining their spiritual path is essential.

Not all are called to be pastors, but everyone has a journey into the heart of God and the congregation. May this be your invitation to move to that deeper place.

Brice Balmer
August 2013

Author's Preface
Sharing the River Journey

For years I've claimed *flowing with the river* as a basic metaphor of Christian life and vocation. I imagine us flowing with the river of life together, yet each doing so in a way peculiar to ourselves. I imagine us each bringing to the river our unique personality, passions and God-given gifts. I imagine our stories intermingling and enriching one another on the river.

I've long been fascinated by the stories of others, both forebears and contemporaries. Through them, I've understood better the themes of my own life and calling. In this spirit of sharing, I offer samplings of my experience on the river and my explorations of its watershed.

The idea for this book was sparked ten years ago by Mary Schiedel's *Pioneers in Ministry: Women Pastors in Ontario Mennonite Churches, 1973-2003* (Kitchener: Pandora Press, 2003). That volume included snippets of the stories and perspectives of 25 of us female pastors in Mennonite Church Eastern Canada. As I participated in Mary's advisory group and read the finished book, I thought: some of us need to say more!

Thus my essays provide glimpses into the life of one Mennonite woman whose calling has—to her astonishment—taken the shape of offering God's refreshment to others as a pastor and spiritual guide.

Along the way I observe the territory through which I've passed, and take soundings into some major changes in the Mennonite Church's voyage of the last century in North America.

My reflections are not uniform in their angle of approach. Through these essays I explore images of pounding surf and of a flowing river, both central in naming and claiming my vocation. Sometimes I focus on a specific incident. At other times my reflections span eras of my own life and the life of the church. The essays are based in my memories and my responses to remembered events. Others may remember or interpret the same events differently.

I hope these soundings from my river journey draw you more deeply into your own story, whatever your God-given gifts and passions may be. I hope our stories continue to intermingle and enrich one another on the river.

Sue Clemmer Steiner
Waterloo, Ontario
Fall 2013

Getting Oriented

Pounding Surf, Many Shorelines

(From a reflection written in 1996)

In memory of Richard Yordy
For Martha Smith Good
For TiM Participants, 2007-2012[1]

My early experience in ministry reminds me of walking along a shoreline with surf pounding in my ears. Sometimes the landscape is as serene as a white sandy beach near Sarasota, Florida. At other times it's strewn with weathered logs and startling rock formations, like the coast of the Olympic Peninsula in Washington State.

But one thing remains the same. Always, always there's the pounding of the surf. The rhythm of the surf comforts me even as its power leaves me in awe. Something urges me to walk alongside it, splashed by the spray. Something draws me irresistibly on—past the next curve, past the next obstacle, to a destination yet unseen.

I came into pastoral ministry as part of the "first wave" of Mennonite

---

[1] Transitioning into Ministry is a three-year program for new pastors in Mennonite Church Eastern Canada initiated by Muriel Bechtel, then the conference minister. Along with David Brubacher, I was a group coach for TiM's first five years.

women in ministry in the late twentieth century. I landed on the shores of ministry towards the back of the wave, but still part of it.

In l987 the surf deposited me on the ministry shore at St. Jacobs, Ontario. But God's call was pounding in my ears long before that. At first it was faint, like the whisper of surf in a seashell. Gradually I became attuned to it. Gradually I heard it more clearly. Gradually I recognized God's call.

I grew up in the Franconia Conference in Pennsylvania in the 1950's, hardly a place where a young girl would recognize a call to pastoral ministry. But if my conference didn't predispose me to ministry, my family circumstances inadvertently did.

My extended family included six male pastors and three female foreign missionaries. I loved their letters from exotic places like England, Cuba, Long Island, and the Oregon coast. My two most intriguing aunts were married to pastors, and I observed them claiming more freedom to use their gifts than most women I knew. And my own pastors at Souderton Mennonite were not remote figures. At all times I called at least one of them uncle or cousin.

Perhaps in grade 7 I began to *hear* the surf through a strange public school English teacher named Mr. Mast. When I wrote a story about loving Jesus, Mr. Mast responded in red ink in the margin, "Feed my sheep…and the sheep have need of many kinds of food. What are our talents? How can we best use them?"

During my student days at Goshen College in the late 1960's, the pounding of the surf got louder. I didn't have a clue which beach I was called to land on, but as editor of the official student newspaper, I did find out what it means to be a leader. Four of my friends left the college against their will after producing two issues of an underground newspaper called *Menno-Pause*. A usually non-directive prof told me that under no circumstances was I to resign my campus position in protest. We need your leadership more than ever, he calmly stated.

And so I wrote careful editorials. I interviewed the president on a significant project of his, upholding journalistic freedom when he asked to review my article before it was published. Don't cave in! instructed our faculty publications advisor, and I didn't. Fortunately, the president liked my published article.

In the midst of this, I visited my *Menno-Pause* friends in Chicago on weekends, and a year and a half later followed one of them to Canada.

As a young adult in Ontario, I began to glimpse the contours of the shore. At Rockway Mennonite Church in Kitchener I found to my surprise that I loved planning and leading worship. As that 1960's-ish church grew up, I was in the right place to sit on its first worship committee, lead a team of youth sponsors, and help shape its first ministry council. I wasn't surprised when seminary beckoned around the next bend.

While studying at Associated Mennonite Biblical Seminaries[2] I found my theological voice with the help of Marlin Miller, Gayle Gerber Koontz, LeRoy Friesen and others. One day after Gayle's class I realized how exhilarating it was to talk theology with the prof in the tiny women's washroom. I wasn't claiming pastoral ministry yet, but I was beginning to imagine it.

The claiming came a year and a half later, in the midst of a disaster. Four teenage boys were killed in a youth group hayride accident. I was the conference youth minister. As I sat in funeral homes with rooms full of grieving youth, I simply ministered out of myself. I startled myself with the recognition that—given the reality of this situation—I wanted to be right in the middle of it.

Afterwards, I sensed that like Jacob of old I had wrestled with God and was no longer the same person. I understood that I had instinctively put on the mantle of ministry, and told the conference minister that I was now ready to enter the pool of applicants for congregations to consider.

In the congregation where I first candidated, the vote did not carry. I had tried to prepare myself for such a public fall from the

---

[2] Now Anabaptist Mennonite Biblical Seminary—still AMBS.

cliffs along the shore. During that scary free fall, a safe landing did not seem assured. Yet it was as if unseen arms of mercy broke my fall. And a year later, when I'd nearly lost hope of finding a compatible congregation, I peered around another bend—and there was St. Jacobs.

I can best describe my first experience of congregational ministry by inviting you to join me in a walk along a lakeshore. Imagine that we're rounding a bend in the shoreline of Lake Erie. We've just spied that spit of land known as Point Pelee, where waves crash from two directions, with many shipwrecks attesting to the danger. Today we can clearly see where the point is, and the wave action looks gentle. But local Essex County folks tell us that the location of the point shifts from time to time, or even disappears for a few years, and sometimes there's quite an undertow.

We step out onto the tip, and oh my it's exhilarating. We're not sure how much farther out we dare go. We don't know where reasonable risk ends. We don't know how to read the signs yet, but for now it seems stable enough underfoot. And though the waves creep towards us from both sides, they seem gentle and warm.

That describes my entry into my first congregation. I wish for every new pastor the kind of guides I had as I learned to read the signs. Two seasoned pastors helped me find solid footing: Richard Yordy, the senior pastor at St. Jacobs, and Martha Smith Good,[3] my conference-appointed mentor. Perhaps more accurately, Martha and Richard helped me cultivate my own ability to read the signs of the wind and the waves, attuned to God's Spirit, in a vocation where the ground shifts regularly. Gradually I found my bearings as a congregational leader.

When I was in the pulpit early on and people said, "Sue, we can hear you," somehow I knew they weren't only talking about the sound system. Somehow I knew I had become a preacher.

When a woman my age was dying of cancer, I made a deliberate

---

[3] By this time Martha had already pastored two congregations in Ontario—Stirling Ave. in Kitchener and Guelph Mennonite Fellowship.

choice to accompany her through this experience. Somehow, at her funeral, I knew I had become a pastoral caregiver.

Then one Sunday after Richard retired, a teenage drama student climbed onto the pulpit in bare feet and jumped off—down into the congregation—as part of a dramatic presentation of Philippians 2. Somehow, as I navigated us through the next few tense weeks, I knew I had become a trusted leader.

Giving Back, 2007-2012

The mentoring of Martha and Richard were invaluable to me in finding a secure footing in pastoral ministry. With his thought-filled, ever curious style of leadership, Richard modeled for me the life-long learning needed to grow as a ministering person. Martha helped me navigate in ministry at a time when having a female pastor was often a new experience for people, eliciting unpredictable responses.

Grateful for that mentoring, I deliberately gave back by coaching new pastors in Mennonite Church Eastern Canada's Transitioning into Ministry (TiM) program as I neared retirement. It was wonderful to accompany others as they found their footing. It was wonderful to see their confidence increase in reading the signs of the wind and the waves. It was wonderful to watch the emergence of a new generation of preachers, spiritual guides, missional leaders.

In the TiM setting, I found myself filled with the sheer joy of ministry, celebrating my calling anew. I found myself immensely grateful for pastoral ministry, the form of church vocation to which I had given 20 years of my life. I found myself walking that shoreline of beginning ministry again, along with the new pastors I coached…

I liken the TiM experience to exploring the beach of the Olympic Peninsula at low tide with peers one is learning to trust, and with guides who ask new questions and suggest new ways of seeing. At low tide, it's safe to go farther out onto the ocean floor than at any other time and see wonders like starfish clinging to rocks and sandpipers skittering everywhere. It's safe to examine the debris that collects on the shore of ministry, and to examine what happens inside of us when the waves crash most violently. It's a time to further enhance our ability to read the signs and to deepen our own grounding in God's love and care for us.

TiM is a place to unlearn things like trying to be perfect or believing one needs to have all the answers. It's a place to give up, laugh at oneself, and simply live in awe. It's a place where the realization slowly dawns that ministry can be explained, dissected and endlessly improved upon, but finally, this vocation calls us to simply live it in awe.

We want to live with surf pounding in our ears, with pant legs rolled up and wet. For this is the place we are called to be, and the work we are called to do.

Claimed by the Conestogo

For Cousin Beulah[4]

Since childhood I've associated bodies of water with refreshment and renewal. My parents and I vacationed at Pecks Pond, a small lake in the Pocono Mountains of Pennsylvania, toting food, bedding and fishing gear to a cabin owned by friends.

Many years later in Ontario, my spiritual director Ruth offered soul refreshment from her year-round cottage on Lake Huron. The rhythm of the waves quieted me as we sank into comfy chairs by huge windows overlooking the lake.

Rivers kept beckoning as well, from the lazy Ohio viewed high above the banks at Ripley to the roaring headwaters of the Jordan in northern Israel.

But in my repertoire of bodies of water, one stands out in significance. It meanders through picturesque Old Order Mennonite country north of Waterloo, part of the Grand River watershed. I've actually never been in the Conestogo River, or on it, but walking along the Conestogo has grounded me in my vocation and helped me claim it more fully and deeply. Here's how the Conestogo claimed me.

---

[4] Beulah Steiner, a Mennonite spiritual director and Steiner cousin, always inspires me. She once suggested that God's ways are like the current in a wide river flowing to the sea.

Conestogo River—Viewed from the Health Valley Trail, looking back toward the village of St. Jacobs, Ontario

The Monday after First Advent in 2001, I walked along the Conestogo River for an hour, starting in a parking lot in St. Jacobs.

Now the odd thing is: in my nine years as pastor of St. Jacobs, I never once explored the river flats. I'm not even sure if there was a path through the flats when I left the congregation in 1995. I certainly wouldn't have ventured there without a guide.

But then Woolwich Township got serious about walking trails. By 2001 a wide impossible-to-miss trail extended from the parking lot by Benjamin's Restaurant to the expressway bridge about a kilometer away. I came back to St. Jacobs to walk it from time to time—a pleasant walk, but not brimming with significance.

All that changed the Monday after First Advent in 2001. That warm December morning, I ventured underneath the expressway bridge and found a much less well-marked dirt path continuing on the other side. I followed the path through a small bush, then through a farm gate which reminded me of rural walks in the British Isles.

After a while I couldn't identify the actual trail anymore, but since the gate opened onto wide river flats, it didn't much matter. I focused on finding solid footing on the squishy ground. Someone had helpfully built makeshift bridges where small streams cut through. Sturdy fences held the cows safely within a pasture up the hill, so I wasn't concerned about misadventures with them. Every so often I stepped right up to the river's edge to watch its gentle flow.

As I continued along the flats I became aware of my internal chatter: "It's really quite isolated here…I'm not sure I should be here…maybe I should turn back towards St. Jacobs." And then, "I've never been here before…I really don't know where I am or what's up ahead."

But another internal voice reminded me, "You can't possibly get lost, for you're following the river. It's here on your left the whole time. You know this river flows to the village of Conestogo. You know that if you keep following, eventually it will take you there."

Later I realized I *had* experienced that spot along the river before. For when Orvie heard me tell this story, he informed me that the trail meanders through *his* river flats, which I'd admired many times from the family's orchard near those cows at the top of the hill.

That walk along the Conestogo, farther than I'd ever gone before, became a metaphor for me of trust in God and the markers God graciously supplies in my own life and as I've guided the spiritual journey of individuals and congregations. Often I've found myself in territory I've never traversed before—or think I haven't— and typically there isn't a wide well-marked trail.

Since that December day in 2001, walking along that section of the Conestogo always revives my spirit. As the sun sparkles on the water, I watch for the osprey, gliding from a certain rock in the river to a tree top along the bank, sun glistening on its wings. I listen for the red-winged blackbird. In springtime I cheer when I spot the trillium in the bush or smell the fragrant apple blossoms in the old orchard. In summertime I step carefully around the cow patties in Orvie's (now Stuart's) lower pasture.

For some unknown reason, that section of the Conestogo connects my spirit with the river of the water of life. Simply put, the river is one of the deep metaphors of the Bible, flowing underneath the text. It first bubbles up in Genesis 2, watering a garden. In Revelation 22 we see it again, flowing from the throne of God—not in an idyllic garden environment this time, but in the middle of a city.

How fertile the river of the water of life is! What sheer delight it brings! No phosphates glisten on the surface of the water. The tree of life is found in abundance on both banks of the river, producing twelve kinds of fruit, a different kind each month. Its leaves are for the healing of the nations.

The same river pops up at various other places in the biblical story, as when the Psalmist exclaims: "God, you give me drink from the river of your delights" (Ps. 36:8). But it's that weird prophet Ezekiel who spins out the metaphor most strikingly. In his vision in Ezekiel 47, the new temple in Jerusalem forms the headwaters of a life-giving stream, beginning as a trickle and expanding into a mighty river, teeming with fish, refreshing the land wherever it flows.

As I walk along the Conestogo, it becomes this life-giving stream. I imagine myself wading in, finding the current, flowing with God's Spirit, being upheld by the healing energy. As I flow with the current, I am guided into the heart of God, and into the heart of God's intention for our world.

For the meandering little Conestogo is flowing somewhere, becoming part of something unimaginably larger than itself. Close by, in the village of Conestogo, it joins the Grand. At Port Maitland, the Grand flows into Lake Erie. Its waters intermingle with others, plunge over Niagara Falls, and enter Lake Ontario. Lake Ontario narrows into the St Lawrence River, which widens into the Gulf of St. Lawrence and encounters the icebergs off Newfoundland as it becomes open sea.

But way back by the sleepy Conestogo, where I first became a pastor, the surf already pounded loudly in my ears, beckoning me on:

My desire is to be in the stream of history
    moving ever more fully towards God
        ...basking in God's steady, sturdy love towards me
        ...moving with the current as it flows
        ...knowing where some deeper currents lie
            and inviting others in.

May nothing distract me from flowing with this stream.[5]

---

[5] Worship poem composed at Loyola House Retreat Center, Guelph, Ontario, 2005.

Nourished on the River Banks

Skippack Creek as it exits the viaduct behind Souderton Mennonite Church and Cemetery, Souderton, Pennsylvania

Between Stink Creek and the River of Life

For our Chestnut Street neighbours, 1950's

When I was three years old, my mom got a phone call from a woman in the next block. "I just looked out the window," said the neighbour, "and there was Susan, marching down the middle of the street as fast as her little legs could take her. I asked her where she was going but she wouldn't say, so I told her to walk on the sidewalk."

Years later my mother was still aggravated with her friend. "Why didn't she bring you into the house," my mom wailed, "and *then* call me?" Why indeed.

I myself carry no memory of this event. I know it only from my mother's frequent impassioned telling. No harm was done to little Susan. Apparently no cars roared down our sleepy part of Chestnut Street at that time on that day.

But even now, 63 years later, I'm curious. Where did I think I was going? Why was I marching "out town" so confidently?

Actually, I think I know. West Chestnut Street in Souderton was my first river of life. I felt safe and comfortable and at home there. People and places on both sides of its "banks" nourished me. My mom and I visited with folks up and down its sidewalks often. And before that, my dad showed me off to the neighbours, strolling with the baby carriage while my mom fixed Sunday dinner.

So maybe when I set off "toward town" I intended to say hello to our near neighbours Old Dan Rice or Young Evy Shearer, or check whether that loud lady up the street was sitting on her porch.

Maybe I was drawn to that big red brick building on the corner where I loved the surround sound of 500 people singing. Despite our kneeling for the deacon's terribly long prayers, it was a friendly place. For one thing, I knew all the men up front. My dad's Uncle Jake, my Uncle Russ and our neighbour Elmer were the preachers.

Maybe that day I hankered for a Summer Bible School story, hoping to smell the glue before the teacher pasted a full-colour picture into my book. Maybe I yearned for snack time, craving one of those little chocolate and vanilla ice cream cups with its own attached wooden spoon.

But my trek down the middle of Chestnut Street that day didn't end at the church. Maybe the memory of my Grampop Clemmer's candy dish compelled me as I crossed Wile Avenue into the next block. Maybe I wanted to visit my Aunt Esther on the other side of Grampop's house, fascinated by her cat, even though my mom said it made the house smell.

Or maybe I intended to keep right on walking till I got to Main Street. If I turned one direction I'd come to Miller's Variety Store, where my mom often held me up so I could breathe on the penny candy displayed in open bins and eventually choose a piece or two. If I crossed the street the other direction I'd come to my dad's feed mill, where people knew I was Lester's daughter and called me Suzie Q. My dad spent most of his waking hours six days a week at Moyer & Son. Mom and I occasionally dropped by to look at the pretty feedbags sold as dress material.

I'll never know where I was headed that day. Most likely, I simply found the gate unlatched and walked through it, knowing instinctively that Chestnut Street and its stopping off places refreshed my little girl spirit. The safety and familiarity that sustained both my mom and my dad on Chestnut Street nurtured me too.

After I reached school age, I found nourishment on the banks of my first river of life in even more ways. Chestnut Street Elementary School met in two buildings across from each other in the next block. By third grade I settled into thoroughly enjoying school, since the teaching methods of that era fit my learning style. About the same time I gained a weekly half hour with my Aunt Esther which continued through much of high school. I cherished her as my piano teacher, but even more as a lively woman, nearly a decade younger than my parents, whose gifts flourished freely in her role as a pastor's wife, or so it seemed to me.

In those early years my world was defined by my extended family, by church and school, by the mill and other local businesses. My mom and I only ventured beyond Chestnut and Main to visit her family five miles away or to undertake our semi-annual clothes shopping expedition to Philadelphia by train. With both parents I journeyed beyond Souderton to visit a doctor they favoured "up the line" in Emmaus, or to eat at the counter of a restaurant my Dad fancied in Quakertown, or to enjoy a lovely field of alfalfa or barley or oats on a Sunday afternoon drive.

Stink Creek—A Boundary

Much of the time my world seemed all of a piece. The values of family, church, school and town overlapped and intertwined. But there was a boundary I was strictly ordered to keep.

On our block of Chestnut Street, behind our house and that of Old Dan Rice, a steep hill led down to "the creek." Officially it was a tiny branch of the 15-mile-long Skippack Creek, itself a tributary of the Perkiomen. Near Philadelphia the Perkiomen flowed into the Schuylkill River and then the Delaware, eventually emptying into the Atlantic Ocean.

"The creek" of my childhood emerged from a spring on East Chestnut Street, near my junior high school. An old Souderton friend claims to have tried to get to the source as a ten-year-old, crawling through the culvert with a candle. In earlier centuries the Lenni Lenape ("Original People") fished in its waters and grew maize along its banks.

But my older brother Jim didn't fish in it during his growing up years, twenty years before mine. He and other Souderton lads called it Stink Creek, for in those days it carried the community's raw sewage. Even after the borough put in a sewer system as a Depression-era work project, my brother caught 40 rats one evening in Grampop's chicken house, just up the bank from the creek.

From our house, the creek was hidden by several barns and a thick shield of trees. I barely knew it existed. Despite my wanderings on Chestnut Street, I never would have ventured down to the creek as a little girl. Nonetheless, when I became old enough to roam the neighborhood with playmates, my mom warned me over and over again, "Don't ever go down to the creek. You might fall in and hurt yourself. And Bad Boys hang out there."

As a school-aged child, I did venture there once in the company of some older neighbour kids and felt very guilty. Then one time when I was 12 or so, an older teenager invited me to go down to the creek just with him. He wanted to show me something, he said. By that time I understood a different constellation of dangers and said no.

I think of that creek, which runs parallel to my first river of life, as symbolic of the way the Mennonite Church[6] of my growing up years understood our faith and practice: you stay safe and you are faithful by keeping certain boundaries. Chestnut Street was supposed to be safe, but just down a steep hill was an innocent-looking no-longer-smelly tiny creek—the boundary.

We Pennsylvania "Old" Mennonites of the 1950's worked out our faith and practice with one foot dipped into the river of life,

---

[6] Mennonite Church was a denomination of North American Mennonites with a Swiss German origin. In the 1950's it was found in Pennsylvania and numerous other states, as well as in Ontario, Alberta and Saskatchewan. It was sometimes referred to as the "Old" Mennonite Church.

enjoying its refreshment. But we also scanned the boundaries often to make sure they were secure, and of course they weren't. Cracks and openings appeared amongst ourselves, and not all Souderton values reinforced ours. A few scenes stand out from my childhood experience.

At school, my first grade teacher thought it ridiculous that I wore long brown cotton "Mennonite" stockings to school on hot days—and said so. My mom was likely more concerned about me catching cold than about keeping a dress code for little girls. Yet I felt embarrassed, caught between my mom and my beloved Miss Andrews.

At the mill, my dad was displeased when one of his business partners decided to enter a horse-drawn antique feed wagon in the July 4 parade down Main Street. Unlike most other merchants, Moyer & Son had never entered a float in the parade previously, due to the patriotic and militaristic associations of July 4. At our house, we celebrated July 4 as my mother's birthday. "They wouldn't have to set off all those firecrackers just for me," she joked.

And in our neighbourhood, the moms and dads didn't know how to react when a young couple fought loudly on Saturday nights. In those pre-air conditioned days with windows wide open, we heard slaps and loud cries; he sounded drunk and people wondered if she was getting hurt. We talked amongst ourselves but didn't know what to do, so we did nothing. We also didn't know how to reach out when a Chestnut Street resident did some jail time, for what reason, no one knew. Somehow our street no longer seemed quite so shielded from "the world."

Chestnut Street Souderton, within a couple blocks of the church, did not escape domestic violence, brushes with the law, or the clash of Mennonite beliefs and practices with societal norms. And at church, two situations and how they were handled stuck in my impressionable mind.

A soon to be married young couple stood up in church—she in maternity garb—to publicly confess their sin. That way they could be married in the church, my mom explained.

And an older couple always walked out of the church service just before the adults took communion. This couple faithfully attended church, always sitting near the front. They stood out because she wore a hat rather than the usual white prayer veiling. "They can't be members of our church," my mom whispered to me, "because he divorced his first wife." That these faithful attenders could not become members, participate in communion, or fully belong seemed sad to me, even as a young child. Why on earth did they keep coming to our church, I wondered, if we didn't want them?[7]

I remember these things from my childhood. But by the time I completed high school in 1965, various boundary markers were under serious attack. Some of them, especially related to dress codes, had already crumbled. But not surprisingly, it took time for the spirituality and practice of "Be ye separate, says the Lord" to be transformed into a full-bodied embrace of "flowing with the river."

Or put another way: it took time for the memory of Stink Creek as a smelly boundary to fade. It took time for us to learn to navigate an ambiguous world where the "dangers"—some of them real, some not—are amongst us, not safely set apart in boundary lands we can avoid. It took time for us to embrace a different, perhaps more difficult kind of discernment. It took time for us to recognize that the renewing waters of the river of life may be found at surprising places, sometimes even in former stink creeks.

In recent years in Souderton, the creek bank of the tiny gurgling Skippack hosts well-kept walking trails and at least one lovely park. And downstream near where the Skippack flows into the Perkiomen, I'm told the trout fishing and bass fishing are exceptional.

---

[7] Similar incidents happened in Ontario and other districts of the "Old" Mennonite Church.

My block of West Chestnut St. Souderton, mid-1970's[8]
1. Home 2. The twin house next to us—the 1950's home of Dan Rice *(facing us)* and Evy Shearer *(facing the church)* 3. the parsonage 4. Stink Creek where it emerges from the viaduct 5. Souderton Mennonite Church, with the 1960's addition 6. To Souderton Elementary schools and Grampop Clemmer's house in the next block, and the mill at the centre of town.

---

[8] Photo courtesy Souderton Mennonite Church.

Feasting by the River
Mom's Company Tables

In memory of Mom

For me, a restaurant meal takes on a special sheen when enjoyed by a river or lake. I regularly request such settings for a birthday, an anniversary, a weekend with friends or any other occasion I can imagine. Whether eating St. Peter's fish on a patio by the Sea of Galilee or burgers at the Old Marina Restaurant near home, my spirit dips into the river of the water of life. And as we linger till the sun sets over the Ohio River or Georgian Bay, my soul feasts on beauty and radiance as well as on good food and conversation.

Yet none of these repasts glow as brightly in memory as those basic home-cooked meals around Martha Clemmer's company table. There by my first river of life I feasted on comfort food and the comfort of belonging.

The night before, we'd pull the dining room table apart, put the boards in, cover the table with cloths, wash the glassware and set out the good china and silverware. Then I'd dust the extra chairs Dad and I brought down from the attic. All the while, Mom baked and cooked. Thus we prepared to host company dinners, usually for members of Mom's Derstine or Dad's Clemmer family.

Thanksgiving with the Derstines featured turkey with both oyster pudding and bread filling. We all knew that the small plate of ham was meant *only* for my brother Jim and Aunt Mildred, who didn't eat poultry.

Along with the meat, my mom served mashed potatoes, candied sweets, baked lima beans, a jellied salad, her own frozen corn, string beans with mushroom soup, dinner rolls, and of course a dish of black olives.

For dessert, she often baked her famous walnut cake with caramel icing or a rich dark chocolate cake with chocolate icing, then waited for the rave reviews. Sometimes she served pie instead, usually a choice of cherry or blueberry with vanilla ice cream. For the diet-conscious, she offered fruit salad and strawberry Jello with Dream Whip.

I still savour the tastes and aromas from that table laden with basic Pennsylvania Dutch food. Yet much more than the feast on the table sustained me. For here I experienced the warmth and comfort of my extended families. Here I most basically belonged. I understand now that my mother's primary sense of nurture came from her connection with her sisters. As a child I felt it—and I felt nurtured too. What was good for my mother was good for me.

At that same table of belonging I took in the wider world. Here on ordinary weekdays my mother and I read the mail—letters from my cousin Betty in Cuba before the Revolution, from Mom's cousin Miriam at the London (England) Mennonite Centre, and from Mom's cousin Esther in Cuba and then Mexico. Here the church-planting efforts of Aunt Mildred and Uncle Curt in Centereach, Long Island, New York took weekly shape, like a magazine serial.

Here my calling to care for the world through the church was birthed, as the six pastors, their wives, and three foreign missionaries from both sides of the family all eventually came to dinner. Their energy rubbed off on me; I rated them livelier and much more exotic than the other adults in my small world. Not all of them ministered far away; during my growing up years and far into my adulthood, at least one of our Moyer/Clemmer kin served on Souderton Mennonite's pastoral staff at all times.

So in our family, pastors and missionaries were not remote folks. I saw them with their guard down in letters and at the family dinner table. Around my mother's table I caught what Jack Suderman, recently of Mennonite Church Canada, calls an "ecclesial vision." My place of belonging easily expanded from my extended family to the church. I came to see my vocation of offering soul food as an extension of my mom's table hospitality.

Mom's Table on the Back Steps

Those feasts bring to mind another of my mom's dinner guests. I don't know his name, and I don't know whether she did either, but a couple times a summer she fed him. Here's how it happened:

A certain thin man dressed in black would politely knock on the back door about an hour before suppertime, leaving the little cart with his belongings out by the front gate. His face looked so old and weather-beaten, and he wore layers of clothes, even in the heat.

He would ask if there was any food he could have that night. My mom understood that it was her obligation to feed him. So she locked the screen door, phoned for my dad to come home, and kept me in the house while the man in black waited outside. Then she made a big extra portion of whatever she was preparing for us. She filled a plate for that man in black, and he sat on the porch steps and ate. After finishing his dinner he knocked on the door, said thank you, returned the plate and continued on his way.

Afterwards my dad launched into stories of the many hobos who passed through Souderton on freight trains during the Great Depression, looking for a meal, or sleeping by the grain bins at the mill. They were homeless, said my dad, down on their luck, and it was good for us to feed them.

Much later an older cousin told me that at Derstine's Mill where he and my mom grew up, they also fed tramps on their porch. With their farm and grist mill located right by the railway line, they had outbuildings where persons travelling the rails could sleep. It struck me that my mom fed "our" homeless man—even in town—because that's what she was taught to do as a child.

My cousin wondered—what if we had invited this man to sit with us at one of Aunt Martha's family dinners? That really would have been something—and much more politically correct. It's a good question to consider.

Yet my mom's feeding of a homeless man on the back steps left a deep impression on me partly *because of* where it happened. To me as a child, it felt like my mom's company table was no longer confined to the dining room. If she could feed someone so strange and different in our own yard, right outside our back door, I had some thinking to do about who belonged and who didn't.

At some point I made the connection between my mom's feeding that homeless man and Jesus' Parable of the Great Feast in Luke 14. That story of excuse-making insiders and startled outsiders fascinated me endlessly, compelling me to write a major paper on it many years later in seminary.

Gradually I grasped that God's banquet really and truly *isn't* just for those who assume they belong there. I looked around, and saw that Jesus' invitation to the banquet puts *me* in the company of an astonishing array of others. Eventually it dawned on me that through the strange and wondrous diversity of folks around God's banquet table, we catch a glimpse of what the reign of God actually looks like.

So in each of my ministry settings I began at least one sermon with "Mom's Company Tables." I always included *both* tables—the dining room and the back steps. In those sermons, the theme of a table of belonging for *us*—so vivid from my childhood—shared space with the theme of a hospitality stretching us beyond our comfort zone.

Preaching in my Own Backyard

For me, the most poignant Martha Clemmer Dinner Sermon emerged from an invitation to preach at my home church in 2001.

Souderton Mennonite had recently completed a major building addition which enveloped the whole block, including my childhood home. Thus I began:

> When I was a child growing up in Souderton, my mother's kitchen was located within the footprint of this new building, maybe about where those exit doors are now. Where I am standing was literally my backyard, somewhere around the back steps.
>
> In the summertime, I loved hanging around those back steps and waiting. As I waited, the clanging sounds of pots and pans sustained me, and so did the reassuring smells of corn fritters or hamburger gravy or apple crisp. And finally, when I could hardly stand it any longer, Mom called through the screen door, "Susan, you can come to the table now. Supper's ready."

That morning I privately reveled in the symbolism: Souderton preachers, including my nephew Gerry, proclaimed God's hospitality from a pulpit on or near the spot where I regularly sat waiting for dinner and where my mother also fed a homeless man.

By 2001, Souderton Mennonite was seriously reaching out to its Chestnut Street neighbours. So I concluded my sermon:

> May the hospitality of Martha Clemmer's table be extended by this congregation in ways far beyond her imagining.

Gentle Breezes off the River
Three Vignettes

Aunt Esther

Long before I knew what a mentor was, I certainly had one—my Aunt Esther Musselman. She was not only my dad's younger sister, but also my piano teacher and the wife of one of our pastors.

I remember Aunt Esther as an energetic woman, much livelier than my parents. She took a special interest in me, perhaps because her own daughter Mary had died at birth six months before I was born. Aunt Esther was an agent of God's care for me, and she didn't expect me to be perfect.

I took piano lessons from her from Grade 2 through most of high school. While I wasn't a natural musician by any means, I likely progressed adequately until heavy school responsibilities cut into my practice time.

We had piano recitals at the local Fire Hall. Each year it was predictable as clock work that Susan Clemmer would forget the piece she had so carefully memorized. Nervousness took over, and halfway through I would just stop! After several years of trotting out to give me the book so I could finish the piece, Aunt Esther finally gave up. She invited me to play duets with her, using the book. An act of desperation for Esther translated into special time with her for me, with all the pressure gone.

During my teenage years, I interacted with Aunt Esther in many settings. I saw her as a vibrant, gifted woman who as a pastor's wife had considerable freedom to use her creativity and leadership gifts. As my youth Sunday school teacher, Esther made it safe for me to ask questions. She accepted doubts as part of faith, giving me hope.

Aunt Esther and Uncle Russ celebrated my graduations with little gifts and remained important encouragers to me. They travelled to Ontario for my ordination, and Esther told the children's story in that service. She played piano when Sam and I celebrated our 25th wedding anniversary in Ontario.

Aunt Esther still taught 15 piano students at the age of 82, and played piano or organ for funerals. She died in 2002 in her 90th year. Now that she's gone, my heart still smiles when I think of her.

She blessed me by noticing me, by accepting me with my foibles, and by expecting God's best for me with a non-anxious spirit.

Mr. Mast

Mr. Mast held the chalk between his fingers like a cigarette. He talked about God openly, but not in language most of us heard in church. Apparently it was okay to cry out in pain and defiance to Mr. Mast's God. Most of us weren't used to that.

Mr. Mast gave assignments in Grade 7 English at Souderton Area Junior High School which most students pronounced "weird." He didn't try to cram grammar into our heads, as most teachers did. Instead he lined up art prints in the blackboard trays, asking us each to pick one and create a story about it. A picture of dreamy-looking young women inspired me to write about Laura Ingalls Wilder and her sisters on the American prairie—based, as it turned out, on a French Impressionist painting!

Sometimes Mr. Mast brought a record player into class, played a piece of orchestral music, and asked us to describe where the music took us or how it made us feel. Later he might tell us that the composer had in mind donkeys descending into the Grand Canyon or the sounds of spring.

I loved these assignments. They drew something out of me which no other teacher had. They introduced me to new worlds, since we had neither art prints nor classical music at home. Mr. Mast also demonstrated how music and images could inspire my faith and help me express it. I had never imagined such a possibility.

In response to one of Mr. Mast's recordings I wrote:

> I was overwhelmed by the beauty and wonder of God's creation. As the calmness of evening grew into the darkness of night, I felt an urgent need to do my best for my Master. This would be thanking him in the best way possible for the unspeakable riches he had just shown me.

Mr. Mast responded to my burst of adolescent piety with an A+, then these words in red ink:

> You are a true poet and have a beautiful faith. "Feed my sheep"— and the sheep have a need for many kinds of food. What are our talents? How can we best use them?

Thus my Grade 7 public school English teacher articulated for me a call floating on the breeze throughout my childhood—a gentle breeze which I felt whenever those family missionaries and ministers graced my mom's dinner table.

Looking back I wonder: as a 13-year-old, did I know Mr. Mast's Bible reference? Or did I ask my mom what Mr. Mast meant, and did she point me to the story of Jesus and Peter on the beach after Jesus' resurrection?

In any case, Mr. Mast's red words lodged themselves at some deep place within me. So much so that I came to understand my call to church vocation in the John 21 pattern:

> "Susan, do you love me?"
> "Yes, Lord, you know I love you!"
> (Well then): "Feed my sheep."

Mr. Mast blessed me by taking my piety seriously, by enriching it with music and art, and by teasing it towards a vocation I took up decades later.

Helen Lapp

Christopher Dock Mennonite (High) School gave me a place to belong as a Mennonite girl. It gave me the only first place athletic ribbon I ever received, as well as the top grade point average in my class. It gave me my first inkling of something called the Anabaptist Vision. It gave me excellent—maybe even subversive—history, English, and social studies teachers. It gave me fascinating friends who expanded my understanding of art, folk music, fashion, and evangelical denominations.

Perhaps best of all, it gave me Helen Lapp. "Mrs. Lapp" married into one of the Franconia Conference's first families of that era. She taught a creative writing class at CD and was the faculty advisor for *The Dockument*, the student newspaper. Through my connection with Helen and with other students who took creative writing or worked on *The Dockument*, I found a place to belong within a place to belong.

I knew even at the time that the stories I created for Helen's class were stilted. I recognized my friend Joyce's stories as livelier and far better crafted. I excelled instead at term papers, such as a massive tome I wrote on The American Negro for Duane Kauffman's history class. Yet I enjoyed writing those stories. In creative writing class I dared to explore and express my own emerging way of seeing things. Helen received my endeavours respectfully, a significant gift to me.

As co-editor of *The Dockument*, I began to imagine myself as a person who could say things which my peers just might stop and think about. In my editorial called "CD Pioneers," I noted that *Pioneers*, the name of our new basketball team, took us back to colonial schoolmaster Christopher Dock, for whom our school was named. I suggested that CD itself was still pioneering after only 13 years of existence. Then I concluded:[9]

> But most of all, each student is a pioneer, weaving his own trail from freshman initiation through the books and papers and

---

[9] Sue Clemmer, "C.D. Pioneers," in *The Dockument*, February 1, 1965 (Vol. XI, No. 4), 2.

exams and committees to that bittersweet evening in June three and a half years later…

Did you expect to follow your present trail? Has anyone passed exactly your way before?

Reading those lines now, I hear whispers of a voice I still recognize.

And in a photo of *The Dockument* staff, I still recognize a certain serious-looking girl with wisps of unruly hair trying to escape her prayer veiling. Helen blessed that too-serious Mennonite girl sitting beside her. She blessed me with her friendly, encouraging spirit. She blessed me by honouring my fledgling attempts to find my own voice, my own modes of expression, my own way of being in the world.

Her mentoring continued as I visited her on trips home from college. At some point the mentoring morphed into friendship.

Testing the Waters

The Falls on the Niagara River—I looked down on the churning waters below the falls when I crossed into Canada in 1969 via the Rainbow Bridge

Navigating Churning Waters
The Goshen College Record

For Dan Hess and John Fisher

There's a spot in Indiana where the leafy maple grows;
Tis our dear and glorious Parkside where the Elkhart River flows...[10]

Thus begins the official Goshen College song. Yet in my four years as a Goshen undergrad in the late 1960's, I ignored the Elkhart River completely. It was a mile away, over by the College Cabin and the dam, and was probably the most beautiful spot in Goshen. Yet I never once canoed on it or even got my pant legs wet from the banks.

But at Goshen College I did get my pant legs wet in another way. I steered a venerable but fragile craft through churning waters, avoiding rocks, trying not to take on too much water or capsize my little boat. The craft I steered was the college's official student newspaper—*The Goshen College Record*—housed "across the tracks" in a non-descript cement block building.[11] During my stint as *Record*

---

[10] "Goshen College ever singing" was adopted as Goshen's alma mater in 1911. After falling into disuse, it has recently enjoyed a modest revival.
[11] Previously, caged mice occupied the space as part of a psychology experiment.

editor during the tumultuous 1967-68 school year, I claimed a voice I still own. I also began to imagine myself as a leader.

Thirteen years later I wrote in a commissioned article in the *Goshen College Bulletin*:[12]

> To recall the late 60's at Goshen College takes almost more energy than I can muster. The times were heady, frantic, larger than life. It seems to me now that they must have run on sheer energy.
>
> As editor of the *Record*, I had the job of analyzing the times while they happened. During that era, it seems to me, both the idealism and the disillusionment of the age impinged upon our sheltered institution—and our sheltered psyches—with a force which caught everyone off guard.

That year the war in Vietnam heated up, spreading dis-ease, threatening to keep us coming-of-age folks from the good life we thought was our due. Martin Luther King Jr. was assassinated, spurring a distressed *Record* reporter to write: "Today the American Dream looks like it is nothing but a gargoyled vision of another time."[13]

And early in the year, while the *Record* staff was still finding its way, four male members of our "publications Brüderhof"—including photographer Sam Steiner—distributed two mimeographed issues of an underground newspaper they called *Menno-Pause*.[14] While I had no part in creating the content, I did unlock an office door so the guys could make page stencils. The "M-P boys" saw their irreverent little rag as "a gadfly…a watchdog…a critic…an extended student opinion board…and general all-around crap." They assumed it would be officially ignored.

---

[12] Sue Clemmer Steiner, "1967-68: The Way They Were" in *Goshen College Bulletin,* March 1981 (Vol. 66, No. 2), 4-5.

13 Dan Kauffman, "A Nation Divided—Will There Be A Sane Answer?" in *The Goshen College Record*, April 12, 1968 (Vol. 69, No. 12), 4.

[14] Copies of *Menno-Pause* are on deposit at the Mennonite Historical Library (Goshen, IN) and at the Mennonite Archives of Ontario at Conrad Grebel University College (Waterloo, ON).

We at the *Record* struggled with whether and how to officially respond. We were not of one mind. After much discussion, we agreed on a staff editorial stating our hope that *Menno-Pause* would survive beyond its initial issues.[15] To do so, we suggested, the paper would need to get beyond "immature sarcasm" and crude language and "choose more significant subject matter."[16] Perhaps we showed our true colours by including in that issue of the *Record* three photos by Sam Steiner, as well as an innocuous signed news article or column by each of the other *M-P* boys. Privately, we enjoyed the unscientific stats on the rise and fall of the head covering in *Menno-Pause*, based on photos from the college yearbook from 1953-67.

None of us foresaw the degree to which *Menno-Pause* could be interpreted as a political act against the institution and its value system. The suspension of the *M-P* boys, applauded by a large bloc of the student body at a Presidential Forum, sparked a crisis for campus opinion leaders. The applause took us completely by surprise. It hit me smack in the face. It felt thunderous and endless and directed at me too.

We had dimly realized that some students considered us *Record* and yearbook folks to be a "self-styled elite." Certainly some members of our loosely-connected Brüderhof were part of campus subgroups focusing on the arts or on popular music or on left-leaning politics. We tended to inhabit the English department or one of the social sciences. And our religious expressions were less conventional than the campus norm. But we hadn't grasped how suspect these various associations and inclinations made us to some students.

From time to time we claimed to want to know what the "silent majority" thought. Yet we were unprepared when we found out. I and other campus leaders with mildly left-wing leanings wondered if we any longer had a mandate to do our jobs. We felt like a rejected

---

[15] We adapted a pro-*M-P* piece submitted by columnist Steve Kreider, reworking it with his participation.
[16] "On Campus Gadflies," in *The Goshen College Record*, October 6, 1967 (Vol. 69, No. 2), 2.

minority.

During those dark days when I felt very unsure of myself, I had two invaluable guides. John Fisher, for whom I graded freshman English essays, advised: the important thing is to stay cool until tomorrow. He informed me that I was not going to even think of resigning. We need your leadership now more than ever, he asserted.

Meanwhile a beleaguered Dan Hess, the young faculty advisor we claimed as almost one of us, called a soul-searching meeting of the *Record* staff. We talked about the minimum requirement for campus publications to continue—the ability to be able to discern the main body of campus opinion and to present it at face value.

Over the next days and weeks, I glimpsed a way forward. I felt determination rising within me. We'd show those students who applauded. We were going to be darn good journalists!

With Dan's support, we set ourselves to it. We began with a double-page spread on *Menno-Pause* which gave due voice to all varieties of campus opinion. Our features on the meaning of Vietnam and of Martin Luther King's death for Goshen students followed the same pattern. I'm still proud of them.

My editorials took on a tone and angle of approach I still recognize and own. My confidence grew as various people—including a few administrators—wrote notes to me in campus mail, thanking me for my editorials and expressing the opinion that we were doing good journalism.

That year at Goshen, I sorted out how to honour my own views while endeavouring to represent the whole student body, and to some degree those things important to the institution itself. Somehow I figured out how to do this while staying connected with the *M-P* boys and other friends who expressed little use for "the establishment." Weekdays I studied and edited the *Record*. Some weekends I visited two of the *M-P* boys in Chicago. Less than two years later, I married one of them.

That *Record* year also afforded me the chance to try my wings as a staff leader, team builder and encourager. Forging a team spirit, making space for others to shine, but also knowing when my own voice needs to be clearly heard—this has always been my best leadership stance. I learned it at Goshen College, navigating a small craft called the *Record* during that tumultuous year.[17]

---

[17] In spring 1968, I wrote an 11-page piece for myself and a few others, chronicling what had happened and my reactions. It was invaluable to me as I wrote this essay.

Plunged into the River
i thank You God

With thanks to E.E. Cummings

I expended an inordinate amount of energy during my pre-teen and early teen years trying to have an emotional encounter with Jesus. I thought that's what George R. Brunk, Billy Graham and the other evangelists expected of me. I was afraid God expected it of me too. Without it, I was afraid I would go to hell.

I thought getting baptized at the age of 12 would take care of my concerns but it didn't. What I lacked, in the lingo of that era, was "assurance of salvation." Why, I wondered, didn't I "feel saved" like everybody else surely did? Why did I have to trudge down the aisle at Billy Graham Crusades time and again, or keep raising my hand at my uncle's mission church? How could I know for certain that my salvation had "taken"?

Both my mom and Aunt Esther assured me that I had committed my life to Jesus and I was doing my very best to obey him, and I didn't need to feel a certain way. But I didn't quite believe them. I wondered how I could ever be good enough for God.

Finally by age 17 or 18, I decided: this is nuts! It will probably never happen for me. I'll just get on with my life.

The positive motivation for my pre-teen baptism had been a budding desire to follow Jesus. Then during my last years at

Christopher Dock, I began to glimpse a form of discipleship much more compelling that the rule-based one of my childhood. At Goshen College my religion and ethics profs fleshed it out. Influenced by H.S. Bender's Anabaptist Vision, they focused on articulating a central core for a life of discipleship, community and peacemaking.

While I liked much of what I heard, I wasn't paying much attention to God at that point. Or rather, I was still busily freeing myself from trying to be good enough for God.

After I graduated from Goshen the crunch came. I followed Sam Steiner, a *Menno-Pause* editor who became a draft resister, to the Mennonite mecca of Kitchener-Waterloo, Ontario.[18] We married in August 1969, and I settled into my job as a book buyer at Kitchener's church-owned Provident Bookstore, where manager Aaron Klassen became an important mentor for me.

Slowly over the next couple years, the reality of our situation dawned on us. We had left our country. We were two children of Menno, disoriented if not lost, who had tried to rescue each other. But the rescue operation wasn't working very well. I wasn't sure if our marriage could hold together, and that scared me mightily.

Then one springtime weekend I traveled to North Lima, Ohio to visit Sam's aging parents, since he could not risk entering the United States at that time. There God plunged me into the river of life, inviting me to splash around and get very wet. God's agent was not an evangelist, but rather a twentieth-century American poet. I heard the Hesston College choir sing a setting of this E.E. Cummings poem:[19]

---

[18] The play *Gadfly* by Rebecca Steiner (7th cousin once removed), based in Sam's story, opened in Kitchener in April 2012. Theatre of the Beat toured with it to Fringe Festivals in Montreal, Edmonton and Vancouver, as well as some Mennonite congregations, mostly in Ontario. In 2013 they took it to Bluffton University and Goshen College.

19 E.E.Cummings, "i thank You God for most this amazing" in *Selected Poems* (New York: Liveright, 2007), 167.

i thank You God for most this amazing
i thank You God for most this amazing
day: for the leaping greenly spirits of trees
and a blue true dream of sky; and for everything
which is natural which is infinite which is yes

(i who have died am alive again today,
and this is the sun's birthday; this is the birth
day of life and of love and wings: and of the gay
great happening illimitably earth)

how should any tasting touching hearing seeing
breathing any—lifted from the no
of all nothing—human merely being
doubt unimaginable You?

(now the ears of my ears awake and
now the eyes of my eyes are opened)

    Those words lodged somewhere deep within me at a time when I was no longer looking for or expecting a recognizable experience of God. It wasn't the emotional encounter with Jesus I had reached for as a young teenager. It was something deeper, more solid, and completely trustworthy. God bowled me over with grace through an artist whose poems laugh, cry, pray and wonder.

    From somewhere deep inside came a completely unexpected intimation of hope, an intimation—no, more than that, a deep knowledge—that I was loved and accepted and forgiven by God. I understood that God was real and possibly even had something for me to do with my life. And I knew that our marriage—to which we had committed in such dire emotional circumstances—need not be over.

    This was not a denial of reality or a glossing over of anything. There was still the hard work of re-creating a marriage on a more solid grounding; still the coming to terms with being in a country that seemed on the surface to be so very much like the one I had left and yet it wasn't. There was still the slow steady work of owning an adult faith and living into my vocation.

But that day at North Lima Church opened the way for new understandings of myself, of God and of vocation to emerge. I had to touch, taste and swim around in God's grace before I could actually believe I was made in God's image. Only then could I embrace discipleship as an expression of my response to God. Only then could I freely explore a call to join God's work in our world.

Immersed In Story

I was chosen before I chose. I was presented with a Story. At some point I was enabled to make it my own.

When I was a little girl we didn't have a Christmas tree in our home, or even plug-in candles in our front windows. But every December my mom and I arranged the manger scene on top of the record player. It was my favorite Christmas ritual.

For most of the year the pressed board stable and painted ceramic figures rested in a box in the attic, each nestled in their own little compartments for safekeeping.

But the day came when Mom and I fetched that box from Sears, Roebuck and Company down from the attic. First Mom set up the stable, then I placed baby Jesus in his own tiny manger, with Mary and Joseph watching from behind. After that I hung the angel from its special hook. Then the shepherds arrived, along with their dog and a couple of sheep. Next I carefully arranged the Wise Men, one kneeling in adoration, the other two standing, offering frankincense and myrrh while the camels waited nearby.

Finally came the star—just a yellow bulb dangling from a star-shaped hole at the back of the stable. But when I plugged in that bulb, the whole nativity scene was bathed in pale light. To an image-starved child, it was wonderful. I spent hours looking at it or moving the characters around, letting them tell their stories.

As a school-aged child, stories of all sorts captivated me. After school I plowed through Nancy Drew in the rocker by the dining room window. And when Mom read Laura Ingalls Wilder to me as I lay on the couch with the chicken pox, I could hardly wait for the next episode. The deprivations of Laura and her sisters during their snowed-in winter shocked me—twisting hay to burn as fuel, eating nothing but potatoes, and almost running out of them.

My mom conscientiously bought the stories published by Herald Press to teach Mennonite history and beliefs to children. I loved Barbara Smucker's *Henry's Red Sea,* especially the dangerous train trip of "Henry" and other Mennonite refugees through the Soviet-controlled sector of Germany after World War II. The true short stories in Elizabeth Hershberger Bauman's *Coals of Fire* fascinated me, especially the one about Pastor Peter offering a meal to the men who came to destroy his thatched roof.

Living into the Story

I've often wondered how within my love of stories I understood the significance of Bible stories.

In Sunday school I struggled to hear my teacher above the din from the boys' class on the other side of the curtain. But in assembly the boys were calmer. We all watched in fascination as the assembly leader stuck Bible people and props onto a special cloth, got the characters to talk to each other, then moved them around into different configurations as the plot unfolded.

Summer Bible School, two consecutive weeks each summer, had its own ambiance, its own energy, and I loved it all. I suspect I absorbed more Bible stories from those concentrated times each summer than from any other childhood venue.

Of course the songs, the full-colour pictures, the smell of the glue and those ice cream cups at recess drew me in. Summer Bible School engaged my imagination and fit my learning style. Recently as I paged through my tattered Grade 1 and 2 books, I marveled at how well the teaching techniques of the day worked for me.[20]

I looked forward to pasting a coloured picture in the book each day, right above the Bible Memory Verse. I also loved the pockets we glued into the book and the stiff pictures we placed in them—wise men's gifts or a sick girl lying under the covers in a bed or the huge "dimes" that fit into the bank shaped like a globe. To this day I can almost recite the "mission story" about Little Wang Fu of China, created in the rhyming repetition popular as an aid to memory in that era.

I wonder when the Bible stories I enjoyed became part of an overarching Story for me, part of a sequential whole. Learning the books of the Bible in order through a Summer Bible School song probably helped. But when did I know that I myself was part of the same Story, beyond the pages of the Bible? When did I understand that as I lived into the Story, it oriented my life, guiding my way? I can't recall any one aha moment.

I do know that as a teenager and young adult, my attraction to *story-in-general* continued unabated. At Christopher Dock High School I reveled in the many novels we imbibed in English classes, sometimes reading long into the night. At Goshen College I chose English as my major. Then in my 20's, while buying books for Provident Bookstores in Ontario, I read voraciously the fiction of my adopted homeland. And in my early 30's, I received affirmation for my ability to restate *the biblical story* for youth as I wrote Sunday school curriculum.

Steeped in Biblical Story and Image

During my 1981-82 sojourn at Associated Mennonite Biblical Seminaries, I plunged into *biblical story* more deeply than I ever had

---

[20] Apparently the Mennonite curriculum "gained a unique reputation among Protestant vacation school materials on the market." It was Bible-centered and related to the (white, middle-class, semi-rural) child's experience. From John A. Hostetler, *God Uses Ink: The Heritage and Mission of the Mennonite Publishing House after Fifty Years* (Scottdale: Herald Press, 1958), 160.

before. I'd known this story from childhood—or at least snippets of it—yet in seminary I found it surprisingly compelling, fresh, and new as I engaged with it intensely. I struggled to make sense of what was happening to me. In a paper written for LeRoy Friesen's theological ethics class, I finally espoused this simple statement: "I was chosen before I chose. I was presented with a story. At some point I was enabled to make it my own."[21]

I attribute my adult love of the Gospel of John to Howard Charles. In his class I delighted in the repeated images of life, light and glory. I saw how story and image linked. I submitted myself to a text so fascinating and complex it defied all attempts to squeeze it into a linear outline. I understood that it wanted to define me, rather than me defining it.

I'm also grateful to Howard Charles for the freedom to explore biblical story and theme in a major paper I wrote on the parable of the Great Supper.[22] (I already loved the parable, connecting it with my mom feeding that homeless man on the back steps.) As I entered the parable in Howard Charles' class, I enjoyed it first of all as a simple, compelling story with a wonderful twist. Yet it also plunged me into a theme embedded deeply in the Bible, where lavish feasts with unexpected guests signal God's salvation.[23] I was so taken with the parable and all its meanings that I compared it to a diamond, shimmering as its many angles and planes caught the sunlight.

At the end of my seminary studies, president Marlin Miller observed about me: "Her strengths were manifest in appropriating biblical images, translation of biblical and theological concepts into contemporary idiom, and her penchant for teaching." He also noted that my use of biblical images could benefit from the discipline of more thorough exegesis from time to time.

---

[21] From Sue C. Steiner, "Splinters from a Journey OR In Celebration of Partiality," for Theological Ethics class at AMBS, December 1981.
[22] Luke 14:15-24.
[23] This theme is sometimes called "the messianic banquet." The dinner guest who speaks in Luke 14:15 has this banquet in mind. See Isaiah 25:6-9 for an Old Testament example.

Later as a preacher, I delighted in recounting Bible stories. As I explored those stories and the themes that emerged from them, I tried to cut and polish each jewel so its angles and planes could catch the Spirit's light in all its power to reveal.

I found myself nodding vigorously when a well-known Bible scholar advised a group of us preachers to trust the subversive power of stories. For stories open things up, he suggested. Stories present choices. Stories are a safe way to suggest things that threaten. Trust the power of Story…

As a ministering person, I did trust the power of the biblical story. And as a person drinking deeply of life, I continued to read stories of all sorts. I can't imagine *not* being immersed in Story.

A Bracing Wind
Miller Time

In memory of Marlin E. Miller

Shortly before Sam and I left Ontario for our year at Associated Mennonite Biblical Seminaries, my mom phoned late one night in a panic.[24] Surely I didn't intend to become a pastor, did I? she wondered. "Certainly not!" I assured her. And I meant it. I did not yet claim pastoral ministry as part of my calling.

That year at AMBS, I found myself in a weekly gathering with Marlin Miller, president of the Mennonite Church side of the seminary. Since we met at 3:00 on Friday afternoons, we students dubbed this hour "Miller Time," taking our cue from a beer commercial popular at the time.

Miller Time turned out to be a bracing but safe setting for living into the disturbing new requirement called "The Senior MDiv Seminar." Six to nine students were to meet with a senior faculty member in a spirit of collaborative learning. As we shared together in this setting, it was hoped that we would grow in self-awareness and be stimulated in our "spiritual formation," a new term which Marlin had to explain to us.

---

[24] I completed my first two years of seminary at Waterloo Lutheran Seminary and Conrad Grebel College in such a way that I could take my final year at AMBS and graduate from there.

The group would give feedback as we each continued to discern our gifts for ministry, observing how our gifts might fit in settings where we were invited to candidate. And—oh yes—we would help each other prepare for the daunting Senior Interview, where our readiness for ministry would be assessed.

We students in the class of 1982 were guinea pigs as the seminary tried out this new way of doing pastoral formation, integration and assessment. As the year wore on, I was more and more pleased that our group happened to get the president as our seminar leader. Marlin Miller had contributed significantly to shaping this new learning format. He could convincingly explain its rationale. But he also had a unique freedom to tinker with it on the fly which the faculty leaders of the other two MDiv Seminar groups likely didn't have. And from that our group benefited greatly.

During Miller Time, the various threads of my seminary experience intertwined as they were meant to, gaining sturdiness and forming, I thought, a surprisingly pleasing pattern. I claimed as my greatest gift of that year the ability to trust my own voice and to see myself as a person able to think theologically. Doubtless the delicious experience of talking theology with a prof in the cramped women's washroom contributed to my sense of empowerment.

In the seminar group, Marlin shamed us into taking seriously our "spiritual formation" assignment of private Psalm-reading and journaling. Surely a busier person than any of us, Marlin faithfully prayed three times each week with a designated Psalm, then read snippets of his experience with these Psalms to us in class.

The nine of us included one Chinese Canadian, two Anglo Canadians, two Argentineans, and four Anglo Americans. We began as four women and five men, losing one woman second term as a female-only MDiv Seminar was developed at the request of some women in the other groups. In Marlin's way of responding to that request, I saw a church leader I could respect and trust.

After eight months of Miller Time deliberations, I still couldn't quite picture myself as the pastor of a congregation.[25] But I kept inching that direction. I fully claimed a call to "work within the church," a call which had presented itself during my ten years with the church-owned Provident Bookstores. The seminar group affirmed me in accepting the position of Conference Youth Minister for the Mennonite Conference of Ontario and Quebec as the next manifestation of my calling in the church.

From Miller Time, I gained three esteemed colleagues with whom I've ministered in Ontario ever since: David Martin, currently executive minister of Mennonite Church Eastern Canada, and Adolfo and Betty Puricelli, long-time pastors of the Toronto Mennonite New Life Church. And as a result of Miller Time, I felt comfortable talking with Marlin in the halls at Mennonite church-wide gatherings, enjoying his humorously provocative asides on the business at hand.

I was sad to hear of Marlin's sudden passing in 1993. Sam and I made the trek to Goshen for the memorial service. On the way home, we stopped somewhere in Michigan to buy a six-pack of Miller Lite to share with certain other AMBS grads who also appreciated Marlin.

---

[25] I also couldn't have guessed that for 12 years I would co-lead (with Brice Balmer) the Integration Seminar in the MTS program at Conrad Grebel, a requirement in the applied studies stream with some similar purposes to AMBS' Senior MDiv Seminar.

A Tsunami of Tears

In memory of Barry Freeman, Bryan Martin, T. Scott Wideman and Michael Wilson

One Sunday afternoon in September 1984, Sam and I listened to local radio on our drive home from a camping weekend. Over and over we heard about a Saturday night church hayride accident in which several youths were killed. My agitation grew, for I was the youth minister for the Mennonite Conference of Ontario and Quebec (MCOQ). In that day before cell phones, I had no way of confirming whether any of "my" youth groups were involved. When we arrived home, three phone messages from Trevor Bauman, president-elect of the conference youth organization, confirmed the worst.

On a country road near Elora, Ontario, a car driven by a local drunk driver had slammed into several teens who had just jumped off a hay wagon. Three youths from two different church groups were killed that night: Barry Freeman (15), Bryan Martin (14), and T. Scott Wideman (15). Michael Wilson (16) clung to life, dying a week later in hospital.

I sat with holy huddles of grieving youth for four nights in funeral homes. The morning of the first funeral, during a steady downpour, I spoke in chapel at Rockway Mennonite High School in

Kitchener. According to my hastily-scrawled notes, I said in part:[26]

> Death never makes sense—unless it perhaps be the death of an 80-year-old who died in sleep after a long and good life. The death of a young person makes no sense at all. The sudden death of three young persons with no warning—witnessed by their friends—is almost beyond belief. This is simply too much for us to absorb…
>
> Most of us did not know these persons personally; we suffer from another kind of grief and confusion. The shock that such a thing could happen, the suddenness of it, the fact that it was an MYF event, the knowledge that all of us go on hayrides and that walking on the road is a part of it, the knowledge that most of us do dangerous things in cars once in awhile—all this and much more hits us. Even if we are not grieving for these people, we are grieving for the precariousness of life, for the preciousness of life…
>
> A lot of people will need to ask "why" and the pious phrases will not work. We will take it one step at a time…
>
> People are finding each other and taking comfort in each other. God has given us each other. God has given us tears to help get out our sorrow and confusion. Tears are a comfort, as the steady rain today is in some strange way a comfort. Being together in silence is a comfort.
>
> Perhaps these words from Romans 8 also bring some comfort today: "We do not even know how we ought to pray, but through our inarticulate groans the Spirit himself is pleading for us, and God who searches our inmost being knows what the Spirit means." (Romans 8:26b-27a, NEB)

After I finished speaking, we sang the camp song *Kum ba yah*: "Someone's crying Lord…come by here." I led us through a time of guided silence, interspersed with petitions for the families and friends of those killed, and for ourselves. We sang *Kum ba yah* again, and I left to attend the first of four funerals.

---

[26] Chapel talk, September 11, 1984. None of the teenagers who were killed attended Rockway.

"The hayride accident," as it came to be known, was like a tsunami overtaking us without warning. Four families were devastated—the landscape of their lives changed irrevocably. But mighty waves also engulfed colleagues and friends of the families, as well as teenage friendship circles, local Mennonite churches, and surrounding communities. The two congregations who lost young people were thrown into intense and sometimes complicated grief.

As newspapers chronicled the shock and distress of local communities, the Mennonite pastors of the area endeavoured to offer care to those on the hayride and their families—and also to those in the car and their families. They struggled to inhabit peace theology in communities where emotions ran high.

As for me, the care of youths and their leaders consumed most of my time and energy for weeks. Without the leisure to think things through, I simply gave out of myself, embodying the belief expressed in a newspaper headline that "God was the first to cry."

When I finally paused to reflect, I understood that the hayride accident was a personal tipping point for me. In the half year previous to this event, I had sometimes stopped to wonder: how will I know when I'm a pastor? What will tell me?

At AMBS I had claimed my theological voice, but that didn't make me a pastor. As conference youth minister I coached youth leaders and preached in churches. That didn't make me a pastor either. During my immersion in the care of grieving youth groups, I crossed over into being a pastor. Here's what I wrote a mere six weeks after the accident:[27]

> There was a sense of having wrestled with God and not being the same person as when I started. There was a sense of simply giving out of myself that I couldn't have if I had had the leisure to "think." There was also the sense that—given the fact of this situation—I would not have wanted to be anywhere else but right in the middle of it. Somehow, afterwards, I knew in a way

---

[27] Sue Steiner, Ministerial Leadership Information Form (MLI), submitted to MCOQ October 20, 1984.

I hadn't before that I am a pastor.

With this realization, I gave notice that I would leave my conference youth position the following spring, to be open to a call from a congregation

Now, almost 30 years later, I occasionally meet up with leaders of the conference youth organization from that era. It slowly registers with me that they're over 40; some are parents of teenagers now. And I experience the magnitude and intensity of what we went through together from yet another angle.

Finding a Ministry Flow

From Showy Lady Slippers to Varied Fen Flowers

For Herb Schultz
For St. Jacobs Mennonite Church, 1987

Each year, Sam and I rent the same cottage on Colpoys Bay near Wiarton, Ontario. In June we always visit the fens of the Bruce Peninsula, alkaline environments along the edge of Lake Huron which provide a habitat for certain rare and more common wildflowers.

This year we found the Oliphant Fen and the Petrol Point Nature Preserve to be wetter and more lush than usual, with most of our favorite June varieties in bloom all at once. By now the ubiquitous Pitcher Plant no longer astonishes us. We enjoy the delicate blue Dwarf Lake Iris as always, and are pleased to see it still flowering as the brilliant red Indian Paint Brush bursts forth.

But oh the excitement of spotting the show-stopper—the Showy Lady Slipper orchid with her pink slipper and three white leaves. There she is, so obvious back by the cedars if you know where to look. We spot just a few of these rare orchids—so fragile, so exotic, needing such particular water and soil conditions to survive. Their ability to reproduce is snuffed out when photographers trample on them in an urge to document their existence. They need the advocacy and protection of the Ontario Federation of Naturalists, as do the rest of the delicate plants of the fen. So the naturalists build boardwalks and fences and erect large warning signs.

Perhaps we 1980's "women in ministry" in what is now Mennonite Church Eastern Canada were like those orchids. We too needed particular water and soil conditions in order to survive and flourish. We too absorbed nutrients underground for years before gaining enough strength to flower. We too needed advocates.

In the Mennonite Conference of Ontario and Quebec (MCOQ) in the mid 1980's, conference minister Herb Schultz and the Personnel Committee attempted to provide such an environment. MCOQ chose not to bring "women in credentialed ministry" to a vote on the conference floor. Instead the Personnel Committee simply offered female candidates where local conditions made it possible,[28] sometimes coupled with prompt ordination to enhance credibility.

Ordination: A Backward Glance

Thus on Pentecost 1987, I was installed as Associate Pastor of St. Jacobs Mennonite Church in the morning and ordained the same afternoon. Now, many years later, the speed strikes me as almost precipitous—St. Jacobs approved the ordination of a brand new pastor when they barely knew her![29]

Many aspects of my life came together in that ordination service. A huge banner and a bright orange bulletin cover proclaimed: "Fan into Flame the Gift of God." My cousin Richard Detweiler preached in both services. Cousin Richard had been my pastor at Souderton when I was a teenager, and by now served as president of Eastern Mennonite College and Seminary. Aunt Esther, representing both my family and my home congregation, played piano and told a

---

[28] Ralph Lebold, previous conference minister, initiated this approach.
[29] The Personnel Committee considered my recent roles in conference-based ministries, for which I was licensed, as pastoral experience.

children's story.

Students at Conrad Grebel College, where I had just ended a term as interim chaplain, offered superb music. Jane Schultz, a former student in my religious studies class at Rockway Mennonite High School, composed a choir piece for the occasion. Ruth Boehm, a conference youth representative from St. Jacobs church, directed the choir that sang it. Her mother Leah adapted the text from 2 Timothy 1:6-7. College friend Carol Beechy read Scripture. Four witnesses affirmed my call. The service went on and on.

Words of Wisdom: Let It Be

That day was wonderful. But getting to it was very difficult.

Two years before I began at St. Jacobs, I candidated for the sole pastor position in a rural congregation. I received a vote of 66%, not nearly high enough. I was told that "women in ministry" was the issue. I heard the result of the vote, by that point anticipated, during a heavy rainstorm. I played the Beatles' song *Let It Be* over and over for days at home and on the tape player in my car.

I had tried to prepare myself for such an outcome. I thought about the possibility of rejection a lot before daring to submit my name for congregations to consider. When I imagined offering myself as a female pastor, I felt exposed and very vulnerable. I imagined myself as a trapeze artist with a tent full of circus goers looking up at me. I knew that to become a pastor, I had to leave the platform on which I stood—the security of working for the conference—to reach for a swinging bar which beckoned me.

But what if that bar swinging towards me wasn't located quite where I thought it should be? What if I misjudged its velocity? What if when I grabbed the bar it was slippery and I lost my grip? What if I went plunging through space? What if I missed the safety net on my way down? Or what if the net fell apart when I dived into it? Then what?

Those were the fears I worked through before letting my name stand for pastoral ministry. I decided I did have a trustworthy safety net—sturdy, yet with sufficient "give" to it. Woven together to form this net, I came to believe, were many strands of support along with the increasing strength of my call. I took courage and reached for the bar swinging towards me.

When the vote didn't carry that first time, I felt bruised, angry, and humiliated. But the safety net held. It felt like many unseen hands broke my fall. The consolation of the Spirit embraced me through the unfailing love of my spouse, the chagrin and good will of the Personnel Committee, and the care of my support group of women in ministry as well as other friends.

That support helped me release my anger sooner than I might have expected. A colleague offered to be angry for me, and I took her up on the offer.

Over time, I got to the place of harbouring no blame or resentment for that incident, for I came to believe that everyone acted according to the best wisdom they possessed at the time. The change which "women in ministry" represented was difficult work for all concerned—for candidates, for congregations, for sympathetic area conferences and their leaders. Some degree of "candidate-as-guinea-pig" was inevitable, and I had quite consciously accepted the risks as part of the process of change.

"*Let it be*" really were words of wisdom for me in that situation. In retrospect, I surely was not ready in 1985 to lead a rural congregation as its sole pastor. For the next couple of years I gained valuable pastoral experience and a broad knowledge of the conference, first as Interim Missions Minister for MCOQ, then as Interim Chaplain at Conrad Grebel College. Plus, Sam and I got to attend a newly-forming congregation, Waterloo North. During its gestation, I had accompanied it as a midwife of sorts in my conference missions role.

Those positive experiences in ministry contributed to my healing. My sense of call to congregational ministry remained strong. But it took a while for me to be willing to let my name be presented to a congregation again. Some churches asked about me, but my first candidating experience had made me cautious. I wanted to ensure that the next time I candidated there would be a better fit.

When in the fall of 1986 the St. Jacobs search committee expressed interest in me, I took notice. As I interviewed with the committee, it became clear that pastor Richard Yordy would welcome a female colleague in an ordained position.[30] This reassured me. When the committee decided I was their preferred candidate, they and the conference Personnel Committee did something else that reassured me. Before my name went public, they conducted a poll to determine the congregation's willingness to receive a female pastor. The positive response was high enough for me to risk candidating again.

I approached candidating differently than I had the previous time. Then I had slaved over a specially-prepared sermon, trying to make it perfect. At St. Jacobs I simply used an old sermon I thought might be suitable. The other time I tried to think of all the questions I could possibly be asked, and have a response ready for each and every one of them. At St. Jacobs I decided to "go with the flow," and did not consciously think through any questions or responses at all. As I preached and interacted with people, I tried to be in the moment, and to avoid guessing at peoples' reactions.

The congregational vote was high enough for me to joyfully—albeit with some trepidation—accept the call to be St. Jacobs' associate pastor.

Varied Fen Flowers?

Thus I joined the growing ranks of female pastors in Ontario Mennonite churches.[31] At least five of us were ordained and others were licensed in 1987-88 as Mennonite Church Eastern Canada

---

[30] The congregation previously had non-credentialed female staff in youth ministry and Christian education.

[31] See the first essay in this book for my celebration of how my mentor Martha Smith Good and my colleague Richard Yordy helped me find my footing in congregational ministry.

was being formed. We owed much to those who preceded us in the previous decade. I hope more of those trailblazers will tell their stories at length, as Martha Smith Good has done recently.[32]

We faced some fascinating and perplexing choices as women new to congregational ministry. For instance, early on at St. Jacobs, a young adult woman asked me with some frustration, "Sue, why do you always wear such dull clothes on Sunday mornings? Brighten up!" I knew I stood out simply by being there. I had unconsciously decided not to let my clothes add to the effect.

After those beginning washed out colours, I became more daring. One year during Lent I wore a purple dress with purple shoes, deliberately donning the season's liturgical colour. (I stopped after a younger congregant referred to me as "her purple highness.")

If we women in ministry then were like Showy Lady Slippers—needing a certain sort of habitat, requiring specific sorts of advocacy, and attracting attention to ourselves because we were still so rare—I believe female pastors in MCEC now bloom in many different varieties. Beginning female pastors certainly still need mentoring, as all new pastors do. How wonderful it is to see female ministers-in-training placed in congregational internships where a seasoned female pastor will mentor them—a near impossibility for my generation of pastors.

But—thank God—in many parts of MCEC female pastors are no longer exotic. The type of water and soil conditions we need in which to thrive, and the way our ministries flower, may have as much to do with personality, theology, spirituality and leadership style as with gender per se. There is not just one kind of female pastor—if there ever was.

---

[32] Martha Smith Good, *Breaking Ground: One Woman's Journey into Pastoral Ministry*, Self-published, 2012.

Life on the River Flats
Staying Connected to the Vine

**In Memory of Ruth Pogson and Omar Martin
For Marcus Smucker**

Before church that morning, Omar had tramped through the old apple orchard down on the Conestogo River flats. At story time, he appeared at the front of the church holding a branch profuse with fragrant white blossoms. Omar asked the children, "How many apples do you think this branch will produce this year?" They started guessing: One? Maybe 5? How about 14? Could it be 33? Then it dawned on a young girl; the answer was "None at all!" This branch would not bear any apples this year or ever, for Omar had severed it from its lifeblood.

Through Omar's simple object lesson, Jesus' analogy of the vine and the branches in John 15 took on enormous significance for me as a beginning pastor. For years I displayed on my desk a photo of a lush vineyard in full bloom. Whenever I gazed at that vineyard I felt joyful, hopeful.

But that photo also reminded me of the outburst of a young lay leader, a businessperson: "Sue, how do you stand it? No way could I do what you're doing! In my work I see results I can measure every week. It could be years before you see the fruit of your work."

These comments turned up the volume on doubts already playing in my head: "What if my ministry isn't fruitful? Is there something else I should be doing to coax bountiful fruit?" On my better days, the question shifted from "Will my ministry be fruitful?" to "How is my own connection to the Vine?" I knew I needed to attend more consciously to my own life of prayer and let God shape my ministry out of it. But how?

Meanwhile, Omar[33] and his wife Lynne kept telling me about their experience with Ruth, their spiritual director. Ruth, they told me, was an Anglican clergywoman who had taken early retirement to devote herself to offering this kind of one-on-one gentle spiritual guidance. I was intrigued. I'd heard of such a thing, but up to that point I didn't know anyone who actually had such a spiritual guide. I contacted Ruth.

A Guide, a Cottage, a Convent

Part of the joy of visiting Ruth each month was my 90-minute drive through the Ontario countryside. I approached her year-round cottage on Lake Huron with ministry cares already lighter. In summer I relished Ruth's perennial gardens. In winter I enjoyed watching the birds flit back and forth between her feeders. As Ruth and I talked and prayed together, the rhythm of the waves calmed my spirit. As I drove home in autumn, the late afternoon sunshine cast a glow on the fields and on our session. In springtime, the green fields promised new growth for me too.

Ruth introduced me to contemplative spirituality. The ways of praying I learned from her fit my personality as an intuitive introvert. Through them, God nourished my inner spirit *and* made it quite clear that a God worthy of the name was going to challenge me as well as affirm me!

After seven years with Ruth, I wrote about my experience of

---

[33] Omar died suddenly of an undiagnosed heart condition in 2002 while pastoring with Lynne at Arnaud Mennonite Church in Manitoba.

spiritual direction for the *Gospel Herald* magazine:[34]

> I could describe what Ruth "does" by saying that she prays for me, brings me back to a sure grounding in God's love, and constantly invites me to deepen my trust in God...Without her, I probably wouldn't have dared to leave one ministry assignment without having another one in place, or taken a self-financed sabbatical...On the way to discernment of these issues, she opened up a new world for me of praying with Scripture and of attending to God through directed retreats.
>
> Ruth has been a keen observer as God has woven the tapestry of my life into some new patterns. Sometimes I find her among the bright threads on the "right side" of the weaving, where the patterns are evident. She always thanks God for the bright threads.
>
> More often, though, I find her on the underside with the tangles, where the real struggles take place. Sometimes I accuse her of creating more tangles! Even on the underside, however, Ruth invites me to see traces of God's leading—traces so faint I would miss them without her practiced inner eye. She reminds me constantly of God's unending desire for communion with me.
>
> After seven years of spiritual direction, I believe more unwaveringly than ever that my ministry needs to take shape out of my own life of prayer.

With Ruth's guidance I started going on silent retreats at the convent of St. John the Divine in Toronto, just across the ravine from the furiously busy Highway 401. I could hear the muffled roar from the chapel.

At first the convent seemed so foreign to me. But over time I learned the Anglican prayer book. As I chanted Psalms to musical tones my mind slowed down; I felt at-one-ness with the Sisters in worship. I looked forward to receiving the Eucharist simply

---

[34] From Sue C. Steiner, "Learning to See Traces of God's Leading," in *Gospel Herald*, April 29, 1997, (Vol. 90, No. 17), 4.

as a worshipper. The convent became one of my spiritual homes. Eventually it even felt natural to eat with others in silence and to not make eye contact in the hallways.

From the convent's site on Botham Road, I took long walks in a residential neighbourhood undergoing gentrification. I tried to guess which old houses had been razed for a new start, and which ones had been gutted and renovated almost beyond recognition. On those walks, I mused how God's Spirit gently and sometimes not-so-gently renovated me and the congregations I served.

The Secret of Bearing Fruit

With Ruth's guidance I developed a pattern of personal spiritual practices which sustained me. They included a daily walk, a morning time of praying with Scripture and journaling, a Sabbath beginning each Sunday afternoon, and an overnight retreat at the convent every other month.

I combined these personal practices with regular sessions with Ruth and with a prayer group of colleagues in ministry. Another trusted companion was the little book *Praying with the Anabaptists: The Secret of Bearing Fruit*. Each chapter offered a brief commentary on John 15, a snippet of teaching from an early Anabaptist, a guided prayer exercise with music, and a prayer of a sixteenth-century martyr. [35]

Not only did my spiritual practices help me as an individual stay connected to Christ the Vine, but over time, they also greatly influenced the way I approached ministry. They helped me remain grounded in God's grace as the only possible basis for my work in the church. They gave me whatever calmness I was able to maintain while leading congregations undergoing significant growth or other change.

I easily imagined myself both as a branch organically connected to the Vine and as one who tended the garden along with others.

---

[35] Marlene Kropf and Eddy Hall, *Praying with the Anabaptists: The Secret of Bearing Fruit* (Newton: Faith and Life Press, 1994).

My spiritual practices helped keep me from the heresy of believing that *my* acts of planting, watering, or pulling weeds would be the deciding factor in making the garden grow. The longer I served as a pastor, the more strongly I came to believe that my first and primary responsibility to the congregation was to stay connected to the Vine myself. Only from that place could I offer spiritual guidance to a congregation listening for God's leading.[36] Only from that location could my tending of the garden stand any chance of bearing fruit.

In real life I am an impatient gardener. But I love to stroll through public gardens on vacation or on a Sunday afternoon drive. And in one of the congregations I served, I anticipated my annual tour of Cora's backyard garden. I delighted in her roses, her lilies and her giant dahlias. I marveled at the lily pads in her goldfish pond and commiserated about her unruly perennials. Then as we would sit in the gazebo drinking coffee, she spun out her dreams for the garden next year and the year after that.

As I caught Cora's excitement, it dawned on me that God spins out dreams for God's garden and invites us to catch them. I imagined myself as a spiritual companion who helps a congregation catch God's dreams. I imagined myself joining in the work as together we dug some new flowerbeds, prepared the ground, and watered tender seedlings in keeping with God's dreams.

The garden image helpfully reminded me that, finally, the beauty and fruitfulness of God's garden is God's work, not mine. At the same time I counted it an unspeakably sacred privilege to be part of this process with God.

Postscript

As part of my spiritual practice, I still make an overnight retreat

---

[36] Marcus Smucker, my second spiritual director, helped me imagine pastoral leadership as caring for the soul of a congregation. Marcus, professor emeritus of pastoral ministry at AMBS, developed the seminary's spiritual formation/guidance program along with others in the 1980's. I met him when we served together on the Board of Congregational Ministries of the Mennonite Church in the 1990's.

every other month at the convent.[37] At a fragile time six years ago, I met up with Ruth there. By then she had fully retired and moved to British Columbia for the warmer climate. But she just "happened" to be in Toronto and at the convent for an overnight stay during one of my visits. I was elated to see her name on the visitor board, and we arranged to meet for an hour the next day.

As we conversed, Ruth's memory lapses became evident. She did, however, remember me and some of the things we had talked about over the years. I believe connecting with her at that juncture was God's timing, even a confirmation of sorts. For by that time I was living into some new directions I had begun to imagine during my years with her. I was now tending God's garden by coaching pastors and by offering spiritual direction myself. Ruth, then my second spiritual director, Marcus, accompanied me as I discovered those leadings.

---

[37] The convent has relocated to the grounds of a rehab hospital in Toronto which the nuns used to administer.

Paddling Furiously
Beyond Hard Work

In Memory of Dad and Cousin Richard[38]

During my parents' childhood 100 years ago, hard work was the necessity and the norm. My mother Martha grew up on the farm at Derstine's Mill. Her childhood came to an abrupt end at age ten when her mother Maggie died. Mom helped her older sister Anna look after the house until their father remarried. As soon as Mom reached legal age, she began working in a pants factory.

My father Lester grew up at Moyer & Son, the family feed mill. According to the tales he told, Dad had to work hard as a teenager. He had to quit high school to master the practical skill of bookkeeping at Lansdale Business College. But he wasn't allowed to finish the course because they needed him full-time at the mill. So he learned bookkeeping on the job from his Uncle Jake, a "tough taskmaster."

By the time I came along in 1947, hard work was ingrained as *the* family virtue, or so it seemed to me. Dad occupied himself at the mill from early morning till late at night six days a week, and he expected employees—especially family members—to work long

---

[38] My father, Lester M. Clemmer, and my cousin Richard C. Detweiler died eight days apart in September 1991.

and hard. He told people he had me dusting the feed mill offices from an early age so I wouldn't hang out at the pool hall. This embarrassed and offended me, since I had no interest whatsoever in the pool hall. Later I found out that the pool hall was one of my dad's own vices as a teenager.

Others in the Clemmer clan and the neighbourhood reinforced the message. Long hours of hard work emanated from the parsonage "kitty corner" across the street. My cousin Richard Detweiler, highly revered in the family, inhabited the parsonage during my late teen years. I remember his wife Mary Jane—no slouch herself—shaking her head at the schedule he kept as he combined the responsibilities of pastor, high school supervising principal, graduate student, and conference leader.[39] And according to neighbourhood lore, Stanley and Doris Shenk, earlier inhabitants of the parsonage, got by on very little sleep. Doris famously irritated the lady next door by vacuuming at midnight with the windows open.

It's no surprise that I internalized a "commandment" that ruled my father's life: "if you don't work hard, you'll be no good." Not only did the Clemmers at the mill work long hours, but so did Cousin Richard and other pastors. I took up the challenge as a student and was rewarded with excellent grades, except of course for phys ed in college and Hebrew in seminary.

As a new pastor I dived into the areas of ministry assigned to me with gusto, and wandered into some things not assigned to me as well. After my colleague retired, I partnered with a part-time interim pastor who came in for blocks of time from out-of-province. At the same time, the congregation embarked on a major building project. I provided the continuity and the on-the-ground detail. I was paddling furiously. I realized I was getting tired. Once in awhile I wondered whether I was being over-responsible. I began to question whether this way of inhabiting ministry was sustainable.

By this time I was learning holy pauses and life-giving spiritual

---

[39] Richard later served as president of Eastern Mennonite College and Seminary. Sadly, he never did complete his DMin degree at Princeton.

practices from Ruth, my spiritual director. The metaphor of me as a gardener-connected-to-the-Vine was beginning to take root. Both my spiritual practices and the gardener image held the promise of mitigating my ingrained workaholism and my propensity for over-responsibility. Then two events unfolded in quick succession which nurtured my budding intention to be with congregations I served in a different way. The first event was the death of my father; the second was a short sabbatical.

My dad's dying evoked and intensified my growing compassion for his considerable struggles in life. I understood that due to health issues both mental and physical, he was unable to live the last chapter of his life in keeping with what he had taught me about a person's worth.

As Sam and I drove from Ontario back to Souderton for Dad's funeral, the hymn "Day is Dying in the West" tugged at my heart. That song reminded me of Dad because he enjoyed singing it; I kept hearing his rich baritone voice. The symbolism loomed large for me, for Dad's day had been dying in the west for a long time. He lived much of his last 25 years in twilight.

When we returned to Ontario, I wrote a tender piece called "Things my Father Taught Me" for the St. Jacobs church newsletter. Among other things, I recalled:[40]

> Dad taught me how to drive a stick shift, to ride a bicycle, to make a proper bank deposit, and to mow a lawn to his satisfaction. He also taught me to drink lots of coffee, to start out for someplace late and still get there more or less on time, and to enjoy a superb field of grain on a Sunday afternoon. Besides these things, my dad gave me a significant gift in each stage of my life, just by being who he was…
>
> During my adult years, my father taught me something neither he nor I would have chosen. His health went into an early decline that continued for nearly 25 years. Those years with him taught me that the value of our life on this earth does not

---
[40] Sue C. Steiner, "Things my Father Taught Me," in *Life Together,* Fall 1991.

finally depend on what we can accomplish…

It struck me that adversity rendered my father incapable of following his own life commandment, or rather, that adversity demonstrated the inadequacy of his life commandment. It struck me that through his decline, which was so sad to watch, Dad learned a quiet confidence in God and a joy in the immediacy of life around him in a nursing home. It struck me that surely I didn't have to wait for adversity or for the nursing home. Perhaps by God's grace I could actually choose a different way now.

That same fall Harold Schlegel arrived at St. Jacobs as co-pastor, a new partner-in-ministry for me. Given my evident need for rejuvenation following the congregation's interim time, I was granted a short winter sabbatical. During that pause, an author, a metaphor of ministry and a Gospel text converged to give shape to the "different way" I craved. They showed me inklings of how to put my still-new experience of spiritual direction into practice as I imaged and inhabited ministry.

Beyond Running a Church

On sabbatical I found myself snowed in for 24 hours in a motel in Michigan. There Eugene Peterson's book *The Contemplative Pastor* hit me with force. We can get sucked into *defining* our ministry, said Peterson, as "running a church."[41]

I wondered: is that beginning to happen to me? After all, a couple generations back my maternal grandfather Irvin Derstine "ran a farm" with his brother. My own father and his Clemmer and Moyer kin "ran a feed mill" (although sometimes it seemed to me that the feed mill ran them). So why should I be surprised to find myself slipping into "running a church?" That descriptor fit my administrative bent, my care about both the big picture and the details, my desire for things to "come out right," and my need to

---

[41] Eugene H. Peterson, *The Contemplative Pastor: Returning to the Art of Spiritual Direction* (Dallas: Word, 1989), 67.

work hard—not to mention my hope of pleasing as many folks as possible.

I recognized with horror how easily I could be lured into the mind trap of "running the church" as a guiding metaphor for my practice of ministry. So I eagerly read Peterson. Pastoral busyness, he suggested, can be diagnosed as "a blasphemous anxiety to do God's work for him."[42] "Being busy" assures us and other people that we're important, for our culture expects successful people to be busy. Furthermore, when we think of our work as "running a church," we assume the initiative is ours. But the reality is that "God has been working diligently, redemptively, and strategically before I appeared on the scene."[43]

From Peterson I received the first inkling that my ministry could be guided by questions such as: what has God already been doing here? What traces of God's grace can I see in this person's life? What has God set in motion that I can get in on or name or encourage? I wondered: if I were to orient my practice of ministry around such questions, how might that change my priorities? How might it modify my need to be busy?

Through these questions, I first glimpsed the possibility of approaching the ministry of a congregation through the lens of spiritual direction: "What is God up to here? How are we being invited to collaborate with God?" I was excited!

Somewhere in my reading during my sabbatical, I discovered the image of the pastor as a spiritual midwife or birth coach. Maybe, I began to realize, pastors are more like midwives than like doctors. As a child I understood that doctors are supposed to be busy, with a waiting room full of people.

But midwives are quietly on the scene, reading the signs to detect when something good is ready to be born. They coach the process as people and groups labour towards new life in the Spirit. Midwives know when to pause for a cup of tea for the sake of the

---

[42] Ibid., 27.
[43] Ibid., 69-70.

birth process underway.

I resolved that as I re-entered ministry, I would pay more attention to when it was right to be outwardly busy, and when spiritual leadership actually required me to back off, to watch and wait, to pause for that cup of tea. In other words, sometimes I could stop paddling furiously, watch for the river current to show itself, and let it carry me.

Resisting the Narcotic of Busyness

In addition to Eugene Peterson, I was profoundly moved by a simple Gospel narrative about a day of satisfying work and a call clarified (Mark 2:21-39). During my ministry pause, this text bubbled up with streams of living water for me.

This text shows us a busy, fulfilling Sabbath day in the life of Jesus, a newly-minted travelling rabbi. He teaches in the synagogue to high praise, frees a man from an unclean spirit, then heads home with Simon Peter and Andrew for a relaxing rest-of-the-Sabbath.

But such is not to be. For when Jesus enters the house, he finds Peter's mother-in-law in bed with a fever. As he helps her up the fever leaves her, and she serves a meal to Jesus and his friends. By now, gawkers wanting to see Jesus hang around the open doorway, and the word spreads—not only is Jesus an amazing preacher, but a healer too!

By sundown, when the Sabbath is officially over, it seems the whole town is pressing around the door. They bring all who are sick or haunted by unclean spirits. And Jesus responds to the need in front of him, healing many.

What happens next fascinates me endlessly. Very early in the morning, while it's still dark, Jesus rises from his sleeping mat, heads out to a deserted place and prays. Surely the place reminds him of the desert where he had been tempted, where in the midst of a confusing array of voices he had been able to distinguish the voice of God. Early in the morning after all that fulfilling busyness, Jesus goes to a deserted place to refocus, to remember what his ministry is supposed to be about.

Peter tracks Jesus down, interrupts his quiet time, and pleads: "You've got to stop praying now, Jesus. Everyone is searching for you. They need you!"

But that quiet time gives Jesus the nerve to do something very difficult. Jesus responds: "No! I'm not going to do what seems most urgent to you. I'm not going to have another day like yesterday. I'm not going to be a miracle worker in Capernaum today."

How can Jesus possibly do it? How can he say "No" when the crowds are right there behind Peter, pressing in? I think he can do it because that time apart enables him to reconnect with the big picture. It enables him to remember that preaching and healing in Capernaum are an authentic expression of his call but not the whole call. It's a precious time to get in tune again with Abba, and emerge with purpose renewed.

So Jesus says "No! We're doing something else today—something that fits the overall purpose of my ministry. We're going to the neighbouring towns. I must preach the good news of God's kingdom there too, for that's what I came to do."

And that's what he does.

Reflections on the Story

I received this story with amazement and gratitude; it was exactly the challenge and the comfort I needed as I struggled to put my ministry on a more sure foundation. Over the years this text repeatedly smacked me in the face with a hard question: Might my busyness be a diversionary tactic to avoid focusing my call? Perhaps even a narcotic? Jesus' example encouraged me to stop and listen for which part of my busyness was an expression of my call and which wasn't. Over the years, it gave me courage to make decisions, however large or small, in line with what I heard.

I kept coming back to this text because I needed it, but also because I suspected it held a crucial word for Mennonite congregations trying to maintain a full calendar of church programs—because surely that's what we're supposed to do, isn't it? In the decade of the 1990's and into the new millennium, this subversive text whispered doubt into the busy bee assumptions of congregations. It gave credence to the "morning sickness of the Spirit" congregations experienced as the pool of volunteers for long-established programs dried up.

This text has fostered the difficult work of discernment many congregations are undertaking these days—focusing their vision, re-discovering their own particular vocation as part of God's work in our world. It has given permission for a year of congregational Sabbath, or for letting go of an identity that fit the church and local community in the past, but no longer does.

Such changed ways of being take time. They don't happen all at once for congregations. And so it was for me as a pastor. When I was paying attention, the image of myself as a midwife of the Spirit whispered wisdom to me, and I could stop paddling so furiously.

The image of midwife, along with Jesus' subversive example, showed me how I was called to be in ministry. They whispered wisdom when my eye and penchant for administrative detail threatened to overtake my focus on the big picture.[44] They whispered wisdom when that voice from childhood instructed me to "work very hard or you'll be no good." They whispered wisdom when that internalized voice was reinforced by our North American culture of busyness. Most of all, they gave me new eyes with which to see God's work amongst us, new questions to orient my way of being with a church. They planted in me new ways of noticing the movement of God's Spirit in congregations.

Despite all this whispered wisdom, a delightfully blunt lay leader declared at one of my farewells: "Sue didn't stop much to smell the roses!" Yet I wonder: how much worse would it have been without that image of the midwife of the Spirit to guide me? Or without the example of Jesus in that wondrously subversive text?

---

[44] I do affirm my eye for detail as a gift to be rightly used.

At Rest
Colpoys Bay

Simply put, the cottage we rent each year on Colpoys Bay near Wiarton is one of my spiritual homes. It's only a matter of time till it's sold, but the home it evokes is by now inside of me. I will carry it with me always…

Some days the Bay shows herself smooth as glass, with scarcely a wrinkle. Then shapes and colours appear—nature gifting us with Impressionist or Cubist art in clouds or trees reflected on water.

Other days the rhythm of rain on tin roof consoles me. The mist receives my cocooning spirit, offering a hiding place, a grieving place, a taking stock place, demanding little. Eventually rain subsides and mist clears to reveal gulls diving, trees greening, waves gently lapping—and a lone pine jutting from the cedar grove, standing at attention.

One morning I happen upon sunrise, pinks and purples first muted then magnificent, casting trees in silhouette. The next day I deliberately rise before five o'clock to sit by the window with my cup of coffee, waiting.

Each morning without fail the light increases. And I pay

Morning light at Colpoys Bay near Wiarton, Ontario

attention to the simplest things: the ripple reaching towards shore as a fishing boat glides by; a set of headlights bobbing along the far shore; a family of ducks foraging near the water's edge—and that lone pine jutting from the cedar grove, standing at attention. I respond with a worship poem.

Welcoming a New Day

I am a lone pine standing at attention
    silhouetted against the morning sky
jutting from the cedar grove yet rooted
    with the others, an integral part.

The bay is calm this morning;
    no waves smashing
    no mist obscuring the other shore.

My gaze lifts beyond the water's surface
    to face into sunrise.
It beckons so brightly,
    promising a new day.

How can I not stand at attention?
How can I not open my arms in welcome?

In a book on Sabbath, Wayne Muller submits that "the Sabbath rocks us and holds us until we can remember who we are."[45] Colpoys Bay does that for me. The Bay grounds me. Almost always I sink into the utter peacefulness of it. It's a place of rest and of spiritual nurture. As I watch tranquil ducks along the water's edge, I imagine resting

---

[45] Wayne Muller, *Sabbath: Finding Rest, Renewal and Delight in our Busy Lives* (New York: Bantam Books, 1999), 151.

my own weary wings; I feel my own heart beating softer and softer.

In this serene state, I want most of all to say Thank You. Colpoys Bay reminds me that life is beautiful. This world is beautiful. I am compelled to worship.

Thus our evening drives around the Bay from Oxendon to Skinners Bluff become for me acts of worship. The ancient cliffs of the escarpment take on a mystical sheen at close of day. I like to stop at Skinners Bluff just before sunset to behold them.

One evening a van stops near us. A kilted driver jumps out, grabs a set of bagpipes, plays a wavy rendition of *Amazing Grace* and leaves. Is he practicing, I wonder? Do his family or neighbouring cottagers object to his practicing at home? Or is he perhaps worshipping? Whether or not he is worshipping, I am. While his rendition is far from perfect, my praise is complete.

Colpoys Bay is also a place of decisions contemplated and sometimes made, of call clarified, of hope restored. One evening we proceed home to the cottage from supper in Owen Sound along the road through Shallow Lake. As we drive through a sputtering little rainstorm while the sun shines, we say: "There should be a rainbow!" I look behind me and see it large and clear, stretching from horizon to horizon.

The rainbow in evening light and the lone pine at sunrise both speak promise to me. Cottages need to be sold. Many aspects of life change. Nonetheless three things remain: gratitude, wonder, and hope.

Fed by Underground Streams

Susquehanna River, from a paddleboat crossing the river at Millersburg, Pennsylvania—a ferry crossing for locals and for settlers heading north since at least 1817

The Clemmer Farm

In 1987 Sam and I bought a small A-frame house in Lakeshore Village, then a 25-year-old subdivision close to the northern boundary of the city of Waterloo. We bought that house because we liked its cozy cottage-y feel; it seemed just the right size for two people and a cat. It also seemed just the right location for me to drive to St. Jacobs and later to Waterloo North church, and for Sam to commute to the library at Grebel.

As Sam and I drove along Albert Street near the turn into our subdivision, we passed Clemmer Industries, an old metal fabricating firm with massive drums and other inventory in their yard. Could those Clemmers be related to me somehow? I wondered from time to time. I knew from Sam, who was an archivist, that Clemmers had come to Ontario from my part of Pennsylvania in the nineteenth century. But I never checked into it further.

Then towards the end of our years in Lakeshore Village, a local history enthusiast asked me one day, "Sue, do you know you're living on the Clemmer farm?" I was intrigued. Abner said he couldn't tell where the farmhouse had been located in relation to our house, because the topography was so drastically altered. He directed Sam to an older member of the "Clemmer farm" family. Sam copied a photo of the farm circa 1950 and gave it to me for Christmas. There our explorations stopped.

But recently, while working on this book, my wondering became more intense. Who were these Clemmers anyway? Suddenly I really wanted to know, so I asked Sam to check it out. After an hour or so of genealogical sleuth work, he determined that the first Clemmer settler in Waterloo Township was Henry M. Clemmer from Franconia Township in Pennsylvania. Henry, his wife Sarah and several children settled in the Preston area in 1822, having arrived in Canada with some of Sarah's Bergey kin. Then in 1837 Henry traded farms with a settler named Erb. Thus the 200-acre Clemmer farm near the Woolwich Township line came into being.[46]

This Henry M. Clemmer, Sam declared, was my paternal grandfather's great uncle! And in case I didn't believe it, he traced his sleuth work for me. I thought he looked stunned; likely I did too.

Unbeknownst to me, I had bought a house on land farmed by my kin 150 years earlier—land that had stayed in Clemmer hands through my own childhood For days I walked around absorbing this new information, reflecting on the strong sense I have of the spirituality of place. I wondered: could such a deep link to a plot of land nurture a person without them even knowing about the connection? Could it have attracted me to 580 Mount Anne in the first place?

I remembered that over the years the house itself had felt increasingly cramped, but I always liked our little plot of city land. In wintertime I reveled in the way so many LBB's (little brown birds) took refuge in the cedar hedge at the side of our property, then flitted back and forth to the feeder outside our front picture window. In fall I marveled at the resplendent maples in our backyard, especially that brilliant orange one. In spring, summer and fall I enjoyed lingering on our covered deck, gazing across our pie-shaped backyard.

I lived on "the Clemmer farm" for most of the years I was a congregational minister. I now imagine the Clemmer connection as

---

[46] Ezra E. Eby, *A Biographical History of Waterloo Township* (Kitchener: Eldon D. Weber, 1971), 110.

an underground stream through which God nurtured my spirit as sermons emerged from my home study, as backyard breezes carried away tension, as I released the joys and sorrows of congregants into God's loving care.

Maggie Uncovered

Odd as it may seem, I was in my 40's and already a pastor when I met my maternal grandmother, Magdelene (Moyer) Derstine. She died in 1916, when my mother was ten. My mom treasured every scrap of memory about her mother, once showing me with great ceremony a poem of Maggie's, tattered and yellowed, clipped out of an old *Gospel Herald* magazine.[47]

During my childhood the few snippets of oral tradition that circulated about Maggie intrigued me greatly. "She taught Sunday school to adults!" my Aunt Anna proudly proclaimed. "And when the chorister at Rockhill couldn't get the pitch, he looked at Maggie for help."

In 1993 I finally met young Maggie and her female friends. A cousin revealed that he had a cache of Maggie-related letters, mostly from the year 1900. My archivist husband transcribed the faded ink and unfamiliar script, eventually presenting 128 pages of text to me and the Derstine cousins—the best Christmas present I've ever received.[48]

The letters revealed a hidden part of my own history. Through young Maggie and her friends, I uncovered a missing piece of

---

[47] Magdelene Derstine, "Keep Ever Close to Jesus," in *Gospel Herald*, August 4, 1910 (Vol. III, No.18), 282.

[48] "Magdelene Gehman Moyer Derstine: Correspondence (1897-1903)," transcribed by Sam Steiner, 1993, deposited at Mennonite Heritage Center, Harleysville, PA.

myself. I understood better how I came to be the person I am. Perhaps most importantly, I glimpsed a group of ministering sisters who gave my own vocation a tradition.

The letters introduced me to Maggie as a 22-year-old Pennsylvania Mennonite woman, coming of age during an era historians call "the awakening" or "the quickening." Hearts were warmed, no doubt about that. But it didn't stop there. Warmed hearts initiated brand new ventures like church publishing, city and foreign missions, and sewing circles.

I realized with a start that Maggie had travelled across the state by train to attend Bible conferences. She was immersed in the developing Mennonite Sunday school movement as a teacher of adult students and of other teachers. She sang in a quartet, presented essays on theological topics, and visited "the girls" at a recently-established mission in Philadelphia, once helping to provide a sewing machine.[49] She knew Aaron Loucks, founder of the Mennonite Publishing House, through the eyes of his "little sister" Ada.

References in letters suggest that Maggie herself considered working at the Philadelphia mission. They hint that had money been available, she would have liked to attend the Elkhart Institute[50] along with her girlfriend Hettie Kulp. Suffice it to say that as new things were being born, Maggie was there in the midst of them—eager, energized, full of dreams, ministering in ways new for Mennonite women.

Essay: "The Sister's Work"

What stunned me most was Maggie's essay "The Sister's Work," published in the church paper *Herald of Truth* in 1900.[51] She begins:

---

[49] Sunday school was a lay-led endeavour meeting on Sunday afternoons. Young men and women gave essays at "Bible reading," a young people's Sunday night gathering in homes. Maggie knew the young women who worked at the (Old) Mennonite mission in Philadelphia.
[50] Precursor to Goshen College.
[51] Magdelene Moyer, "The Sisters' Work," in *Herald of Truth*, April 1, 1900. *Herald of Truth*, begun by John F. Funk in Elkhart, IN. in 1864 and privately-owned, was one of the precursors

Some think that the sister's work is merely to look after the needs of the family...If this be our work, let us do it "heartily as unto the Lord."

Then she notes that in studying the Scriptures, "we find there is also other work which the sisters may do."

Maggie's argument parallels that used by Holiness groups in her era to sanction women pastors. She quotes the prophet Joel on God's Spirit being poured out on all flesh, so that "your sons and daughters shall prophesy" (Joel 2:28). Surely, my 22-year-old grandmother contended, both men and women did receive the Holy Spirit on the day of Pentecost. Therefore:

> God says they shall prophesy, sisters included. If we are born again, have the love of Christ in our hearts, and are filled with His Spirit, let us obey. Philip the evangelist had four daughters, virgins, which did prophesy (Acts 21:8-9). Prophesying is speaking to edification, exhortation and comfort (1 Cor. 14:3).

In the rest of the essay Maggie exhorts women to use their talents, whatever they may be, citing the example of Dorcas, who sewed garments for the poor, and Mary Magdalene, who was a missionary to the disciples on Easter morning. These examples are carefully chosen, for at this time young women were leaving their sheltered rural Mennonite communities to head to India, and sewing circles were forming in local congregations to support their mission work.

Maggie concludes her article with these words:

> As the Lord leads, let us follow. Let us be earnest in His work, so that He can say of us, "She hath done what she could."

Fall 1900: Crucial Time of Decision

Six months after Maggie's heady essay on "The Sister's Work" was published, she stopped travelling around to Bible conferences and city missions. Several letters show the agony of her decision making,

---

of the church-owned *Gospel Herald*, begun by Aaron Loucks as *Gospel Witness* in 1905.

the sorting out of her call. In October 1900 she returned home from an extended trip to western Pennsylvania at the behest of her mother, who said her help was needed in the butchering business.

Even Maggie's young sister Alma contributed to the "Maggie come home" campaign with this gem: [52]

> I thought write and tell you that I want you to come home because Ella May is going next week and I can not see how we can spare you and I don't like mamma too work so hard then I might have to stay home from school...And I don't want to stay home from school and become so dumb... Please come.

Maggie sought counsel from Irvin A. Derstine, with whom she exchanged six increasingly tender letters between August 30 and October 17. After she'd been gone a little more than a month, Irvin wrote:[53]

> You ask the question what you should do about staying out there. I think you ask the wrong party if you ask me. I might still be too selfish to answer it...But the best is to find out God's will and then obey.

Maggie requested ten dollars from her parents for the journey and came home. Within four months she married my grandfather Irvin, who operated a gristmill on his family farm miles away—too far way to assist with her family's butchering!

I'm fascinated that Maggie only informed one of her correspondents about her upcoming marriage. The others learned of it by the grapevine, and wrote in surprise with their congratulations. In a letter after the wedding, Ada Loucks mentioned that Maggie had written (in a missing letter) of her recent "dark hours." I wonder what those "dark hours" were about. I wonder why she didn't tell "the girls" about her upcoming marriage. I wonder if she thought

---

[52] Alma Moyer to Magdelene Moyer in "Correspondence," September 19, 1900, 108 (grammar uncorrected). As a child, I remember visiting (my mom's) Aunt Alma and Uncle Harvey Moyer. I thought of Aunt Alma as a nice old lady.

[53] Irvin A. Derstine to Magdelene Moyer in "Correspondence," September 30, 1900, 9 (grammar corrected). Maggie's letter to Irvin is missing.

she had somehow let down the cause…

Maggie as Metaphor

As a married farm woman, Maggie taught Sunday school when she could, gave the pitch when the chorister couldn't get it, and published that one poem, "Keep Ever Close to Jesus." She birthed three children who lived and two who died; the last baby took her also at the age of 39. I'm her only granddaughter to survive infancy.

So what do I make of her life? How do I receive her? How do I put together her young adult eagerness, her excitement about new ways of ministering, with her settled life as a farm woman?

I like to imagine Maggie as an underground stream nourishing my own call. Surely her life—both before and after her marriage—contributed to the high value placed on church vocation amongst my Derstine kin. Five of Maggie's descendants are currently active or retired pastors.

At the same time I receive Maggie as metaphor—a metaphor of what happened to a whole generation of energetic Mennonite women who came of age around the turn of the twentieth century. They cared deeply about the church. They had a lot to offer. But something happened. And it wasn't only that many of them "settled down," married and raised families back home in their mostly rural Mennonite communities.

Something else happened. Many of the dreams of that generation of women were stillborn. For by the mid 1920's the religious climate had changed. Fundamentalism overtook the Holiness movement as a major theological influence, with much debate about appropriate roles for women. Following two decades of institution-building, centralization under male leadership became the order of the day. So in most places in the (Old) Mennonite church, the "new ways" of women ministering were replaced, sometimes forcibly, by older, less threatening ways.[54]

---

[54] In 1926-28, the quasi-independent Woman's Missionary Society was taken over by an all-male Mission Board and given a much-reduced mandate. Sam's grandmother Martha

Given all this, I came to see my vocational call as continuing the trajectory of my grandmother and others of her era, as I ministered in ways and with a freedom which they couldn't. Yet discovering Maggie also fed into my sense of fragility about the ongoing place of women in church leadership. Shortly after reading the Maggie letters, I offered a reflection piece called "Keeping the Dream Alive" to the *MCC Women's Concerns Report*. I wrote in part:[55]

> Often I've wondered about the generation of women who are set to come of age at the turn of the 21st century. Will their dreams of full participation in the church be stillborn?

I took courage in an event of 1992 momentous for me—the ordination of Ruth Boehm at Bethel Mennonite Church in Winnipeg.[56] I took courage in that:

> Ruth is a second generation, late-20th century woman in ministry. That is to say, she is a woman in ministry mentored by another woman in ministry—namely me…Even while my own dreams were fragile, I embodied new possibilities for Ruth and others. Ruth's ordination gives me the courage to say, "We are more than a one-generation aberration…We will continue to use our gifts of ministry alongside those of men…so that new things can continually be born amongst us."

Ministering Sisters

So with part of myself I receive Maggie as metaphor, and her early experience as an underground stream nourishing my call to ministry. But there's also another part of me. That part of me cringed when I read the letter Maggie's maternal grandmother wrote to her when Maggie had at least one small child. Maggie's grandma and namesake Magdelena wrote:[57]

(Whitmer) Steiner's church-wide leadership position ceased to exist when this takeover happened. She died of cancer a year later.

[55] Sue C. Steiner, "Keeping the Dream Alive," in *MCC Women's Concerns Report*, July-August 1993, 11-12.

[56] Ruth is currently pastor of Faith Mennonite Church in Leamington, ON.

[57] Maggie's grandmother was the locally-known poet Magdelena Gross Fly. Letter to "Dear

> I wish I was there every Sunday to take care of dear little Anna, and then you could have a class and be a worker in the vineyard of Christ as you used to do in times past.

This well-meaning wish for Maggie, with its specific interpretation of what it means to be "a worker in the vineyard of Christ," unsettled me. I didn't like the hierarchy of ministries my great great-grandmother implied. With my late 20th-century sensibilities, I wanted to protect Maggie from any hint of having made a lesser choice. I wanted to honour the kind of "work in Christ's vineyard" she chose as a farm wife, mother and occasional Sunday school teacher, writer and pitch-giver.

Through Sam's research I recently came upon the term "ministering sisters," used by a Mennonite group in Maggie's era to describe women who were church planters and pastors.[58] Janet Douglas, the first Mennonite woman evangelist and pastor in North America, was about the age of my decision-making grandmother when she ministered to her congregation in Dornoch, Ontario.[59]

I like the term ministering sisters. I like the feel of it; I like the sound of it. But I want to expand it greatly. I want to expand it to cover young and not so young women who dream dreams like Maggie. I want it to include pastor's wives such as my Aunt Esther and my Aunt Mildred, female pastors in MCEC, the sisters of St. John the Divine in Toronto, Priscilla of the New Testament, and countless other women with a call to church vocation throughout the centuries.

As long as there is a church—or even if church at some point takes a form we wouldn't recognize now—I believe there will be eager, energized, sometimes long-suffering ministering sisters.

Grand children," in "Correspondence," May 190?, 113-114.
[58] The Mennonite Brethren in Christ, now the Evangelical Missionary Church in Canada, the Missionary Church in the USA, and the Bible Fellowship Church in PA.
[59] Sam Steiner, "Hall, Janet Douglas (1863-1946)" in *Global Anabaptist Mennonite Encyclopedia Online*. http://www.gameo.org/encyclopedia/contents/hall_janet_douglas_1863_1946.

Exploring the Watershed

Susquehanna River—Island near McKee's Half Falls north of Harrisburg, Pennsylvania

The Susquehanna
Discovering a Vast Watershed

Sam and I journey to my childhood home in Pennsylvania at least twice a year, passing through territory nourishing to my eyes and my spirit. On Canadian Thanksgiving weekend, a favorite travelling time, the maples, oaks and sumac display their most brilliant hues. In winter, snow graces the gently rolling slopes of New York's Southern Tier. And in April, when I'm desperate for spring, Pennsylvania's budding trees and flowering bushes slowly thaw my wintry spirit.

I anticipate a glimpse of the Susquehanna River in any season. Astonishingly, we encounter it on each of the four different routes we favour between Waterloo and Souderton:

Route #1: If we detour two hours east to visit friends in Cooperstown, we find ourselves at the headwaters of the Susquehanna—a small stream flowing out of Lake Otsego, just deep and wide enough to host a 70-mile canoe race. Early one morning we stood there, hugging cups of coffee, watching canoes glide out of the mist with calls of Hep! Hep! Hep! as Cooperstown's annual Memorial Day Regalia began.

Route #2: If we decide speed is of the essence, we drive beside a small babbling stream—also the Susquehanna—as we skirt the southern border of New York on the interstate, anticipating our turn south into Pennsylvania at Binghamton.

Route #3: If it's a clear day and we feel like meandering, we dip into Pennsylvania at Waverly. We marvel at the Susquehanna—by now a substantial river—snaking its way between Towanda and Tunkhannock, cutting deep lateral gashes through the so-called Endless Mountains as it executes a huge S curve.

Route #4: If we're hankering to stop in Lancaster on our way to Souderton, we turn south into Pennsylvania near Corning. On this route we cross over the Susquehanna in Williamsport. Then as we drive along Route 15 north of Harrisburg, we find the Susquehanna again flowing beside us, a wide river hurling itself over McKees Half Falls on its way to the Chesapeake Bay.

For years I simply enjoyed these individual sightings of the Susquehanna, until finally it occurred to me to wonder about some things. How, I wondered, could the same river be at so many places on our travelling routes? How could the peaceful little stream that hosts an annual canoe race be the same powerful river that cuts a spectacular zigzag course through the Endless Mountains and rushes over McKee Half Falls near that Mennonite bakery we enjoy? How could this peaceful little stream gather enough water along its way to contribute two-thirds of the volume of the Chesapeake Bay?

How could I have encountered this river on four different routes without grasping the hugeness of its watershed—or even quite registering that all these sightings were indeed the same river? And how mysterious is it that 190 years ago, Uncle Henry Clemmer plodded along this same winding river, cutting through the mountain passes we see near Towanda in his journey to a hoped-for promised land in Upper Canada?

Intrigued, I began reading the signs at the Susquehanna's source and at high lookouts in the Endless Mountains. They confirmed that the Susquehanna's watershed encompasses half of the territory through which I have travelled back and forth these 44 years. By consulting a map, I finally grasped that the Susquehanna has a north branch and a west branch which come together south of Williamsport, forming the longest river on the American east coast.

Roadside signs and my conversations with locals confirmed an increasing desire to care for the river and its watershed. How would mussels or carp in Lake Otsego affect the river downstream, folks from Cooperstown wondered? How would fracking—so tempting for subsistence farmers—affect the groundwater?

The Watershed We're In

"You always need to know which watershed you're in" said a Cooperstown local one day as we stood at the headwaters of the Susquehanna. "That will tell you which way all the rivers are flowing."

As I thought about her comment and about my slowly-dawning awareness of the Susquehanna, I reflected on how long it's taken me to grasp the scope and diversity of another watershed—the watershed of the coming reign of God. That's the watershed in which I've chosen to live and move and have my being. As with the Susquehanna, the streams in this watershed all flow in the same direction—into the heart of God and the heart of God's purposes for our world.

I've glimpsed the reign of God at places expected and unexpected—around my mom's dinner table, at an Easter Vigil service at Notre Dame University, in the Waterloo Generations Thrift Shop. I've said "ah yes, here it is!" while baptizing a young adult or leading a Thanksgiving service in a low-income apartment building or offering a fiction book club in our local women's prison. I've encountered some sightings so small and innocuous I've almost missed them. Others have cut a zigzag course through sheer rock, impossible to miss.

As a pastor, I've wanted God to give us in Mennonite congregations eyes to marvel at the vastness of the watershed, at the unpredictability of the sightings of God's coming reign. At the same time I've wanted us to find the river's deep channel and flow with the current. I've wanted us to go deep and wide. I've wanted us to take good care of the part of the river entrusted to us for the sake of the whole watershed.

I've wanted God to enlighten our eyes through worship, preaching, one-on-one conversation, congregational discernment—and through whatever other openings the Spirit pleases. I've wanted us to connect what happens in church with what happens in our communities and our daily lives

I've wanted the coming reign of God to be as surprisingly evident to us, as vast in its scope, as ubiquitous in its appearance, as the Susquehanna is for me on my journey between homes.

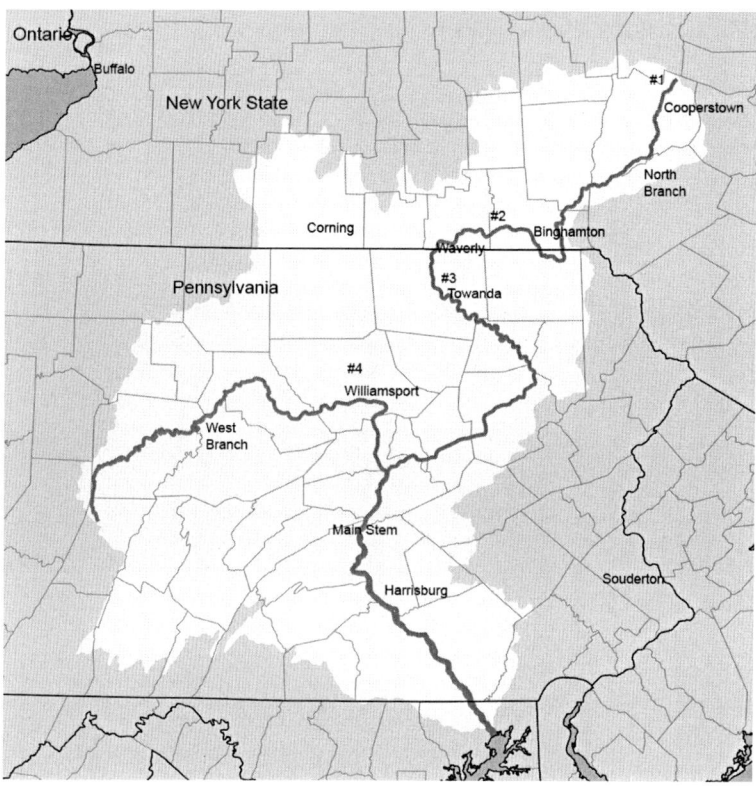

The Susquehanna Watershed[60]

---

[60] Based on Karl Musser, "The Susquehanna Watershed," in *Wikipedia, the free encyclopedia.* https://en.wikipedia.org/wiki/File:Susq.png.

Rituals on the River
Then and Now

**In gratitude for Souderton Mennonite Church, 1950's
For Marlene Kropf**

I remember it like this:

In my childhood congregation we celebrated one Sunday of Easter, and it was glorious. We greeted one another with the only call and response I recall from our worship in that era:

"The Lord is risen."

"He is risen indeed!"

Each year I reveled in the Easter carols, especially the tempo changes and sheer energy of *Low in the grave He lay*. It began so sad and slow:

> Low in the grave He lay, Jesus my Savior!
> Waiting the coming day—Jesus my Lorrrrd!

We held that last note for a long time, gaining momentum for the high speed romp of 500 unaccompanied voices through the refrain:

> Up from the grave He arose, (He arose,)
> with a mighty triumph o'er His foes! (He arose!)
> He arose a Victor from the dark domain,
> and He lives forever with His saints to reign.
> He arose! (He arose!)

> He arose! (He arose!)
> Hallelujah! Christ arose!⁶¹

On that morning, we dared to joy. We sang as fast as we possibly could, so fast I wondered whether the chorister would lose control of us. Joy overtook the usual austere tone of our worship. And then, abruptly, Easter was over for another year.

My impression as a child was that, except for the singing, church centered mostly on listening to words—an endurance test for young bodies and minds. My dad spoke sternly to me about my behaviour during the deacon's long prayer, and took me out to spank me at least once. During that prayer we knelt backwards, so my attention wandered to the soles of people's shoes or the shape of their rear ends, rather than remaining with the deacon's sincere words.

Our red brick meetinghouse, built in 1915, was deliberately unadorned. The white walls, wooden benches and windows with plain glass were meant to keep us focused on God rather than on our surroundings. The only worship visual I recall was Preacher Elmer Moyer's replica of the Israelite tabernacle, which was somehow connected, said my mother, to certain understandings of what will happen when the world ends and Jesus comes again.

Besides the singing, my favorite part of worship was the benediction. I liked it because it signaled "You can go now!" But beyond that, the tender tone of the preacher's voice and his quaint King James Bible words caught my attention. Phrases like "that great Shepherd of the sheep" and "the peace of God which passeth all understanding" comforted me.

The benediction from Jude 24-25 especially cheered me. Apparently, God was able to "present me faultless before the presence of His glory with exceeding joy." Me? A little girl who couldn't even kneel quietly during the deacon's prayer!

---

⁶¹ Robert Lowry, "Christ Arose," *Life Songs #2* (Scottdale: Mennonite Publishing House, 1938), 284.

Vast Realities Condensed

I doubt that I paid much attention to the ordinances of my childhood church until I participated in them at age 12. My baptism in 1959 also plunged me into communion, foot washing, the holy kiss and the wearing of the prayer veiling. By experiencing these ordinances, I was initiated into Mennonite ritual as practiced at that time.[62]

The hot summer day of my Christian initiation I wore a navy long-sleeved dress. I was the youngest in the long line of 11 waiting to be baptized by my dad's Uncle Jake. Whether by happenstance or design, my turn came last.

All my senses were heightened that day. I remember my fear that I would faint from kneeling so long in the heat and then my baptism wouldn't "take." I remember how hard the bare wood floor felt under my knees. I remember my concern that the water poured on my head would dent my new prayer veiling. I remember the smell of sweat and the trickle of water making its way down my hot face. I remember my dread of the "holy kiss" I would receive from the deacon's wife.

At the same time I recall asking for baptism out of a tender heart. I wanted to know for sure that my sins were forgiven. I wanted to follow Jesus. I understood that baptism in and of itself couldn't save me. Yet I wondered if more was going on here than they told us. (Much later, John Rempel's simple statement in *Minister's Manual* resounded within me: "Rituals condense vast realities into simple gestures."[63])

Baptism meant that I could now participate—or rather was obliged to take part—in communion. And with communion came "counsel meeting" and "foot washing." During "counsel meeting" I shook hands with the ministers and the deacon, looked them in the eye and nodded to indicate that I was right with God and with

---

[62] *Mennonite Confession of Faith*, adopted five years after my baptism, listed these and three other ordinances (ordination, anointing and marriage) as "symbols of Christian truths to be observed permanently by the church." (Scottdale: Herald Press,1963), 16.
[63] John Rempel, ed., *Ministers' Manual* (Newton: Faith and Life Press,1998), 62.

everyone in the congregation. (But how could a 12-year-old know for sure? How could anybody?)

As for foot washing, Aunt Esther came to my rescue by offering to be my partner that first time. I was proud to "wash feet" with her as a symbol of humility and loving service. I liked sitting across from her over a basin of water and having her gently slosh water first over one of my stockinged feet then the other, drying them with a white towel. I was fine doing the same for her because I knew if I didn't get it quite right it would be okay. Nor was I embarrassed to exchange a kiss of peace with Aunt Esther. But after that first time I always "washed feet" with a girlfriend, so as not to get stuck with some old lady I didn't know who would actually expect me to take off my nylons, rather than just sloshing water over them.

I recall nothing about my first communion, although I'm certain we no longer used Harvey Freed's dandelion wine, as the congregation did in earlier years. I don't know how the elements were distributed. Nor do I have any recollection of what communion meant to me. I suspect I was just relieved to find a ritual I could do properly, without drawing undue attention to myself.

Gifts for My River Journey

The worship which encircled my childhood shaped me profoundly, offering gifts for my own journey and forming in me sensibilities which have informed my adult practice of ministry.

Worship at Souderton Mennonite fostered in me an adult love of worship spaces with simple elegance. At Waterloo North I cherished the stone wall behind the pulpit, composed of stones brought from the many home communities and global church connections of its members. At Rockway when we met in the school library, I loved the strength and beauty of the evergreen trees viewed through the large windows. At Rockway Church now, in the building we share with Zion United, I appreciate the translucent glass windows with their simple floral design.

My childhood ways of bodily participating in worship—

singing in four-part harmony, kneeling together to pray—were in fact powerful enactments of being the body of Christ. Much later I understood that in singing we respond to God as embodied selves, mysteriously connected with everyone else as our voices blend in harmony. Much later a teenager remarked that when we pray together as a congregation, it's as if there's an invisible circle around the room, and all our prayers "go up to God as one prayer."

Our dress code in my childhood worship, tending towards austerity, led me to expect that as a Christian I was to be "different" in some ways from the surrounding culture. While I now use other markers to indicate the church as a "contrast society," I take the point, and sometimes wonder whether some visible symbols could help us.

I reached out for baptism at a young age, hoping that it could somehow lead me deeper into the living water my spirit craved. The infrequency of communion, along with the serious counsel meeting and the strange acted parable of foot washing, signaled for me communion's importance. Looking back I'm aware of how the rituals of baptism, foot washing, communion and the holy kiss engaged my sense of taste, touch and smell (!), otherwise absent in Mennonite worship of that era.

Much later as a pastor, officiating at baptism and communion was such a holy privilege. I delighted in the sheer physicality—the fragrance of the bread and grape juice, the breaking of a loaf of bread held high, the trickle of baptismal water seeping through my fingers. I reveled in the layered meanings of these signs. I hoped they meant as much or even more to others as they did to me.

Liturgical Renewal

When I became a pastor in 1987 liturgical renewal was already underway, drawing music, drama, the arts and ritual into worship in ways new to Mennonites. I'd already tasted it in the 1970's as a member of Rockway Church's worship committee. In 1981-82, my spirit feasted in chapel services at seminary. The worship

I experienced there refreshed me, so when I became a pastor I wanted to bring that refreshment to the congregations I served. But I wanted to do so while honouring Mennonite simplicity and theological understandings.

A highlight of my seminary year was the Easter Vigil Service at the Sacred Heart Cathedral at Notre Dame University. A carload of us drove an hour to South Bend for the service. Through it God astonished my being, unblocking many channels all at once. I experienced God drawing me to herself through light and darkness, sound and silence, space, colour and ritual in ways beyond my imagining.

The three-hour Vigil had everything—two separate candle lighting services, Scripture reading with choral responses, a homily, an adult baptism at midnight, a renewal of our baptismal vows, and of course the celebration of the bread and the cup. It enveloped us 2000 worshippers completely, dipping us deep into Easter.

As we re-emerged into the northern Indiana night air at 1:00 a.m., it struck me that all our senses had been engaged—by candlelight slowly rolling towards us, its glow filling the vast dome; by the singing of the cantor and the babbling of baptismal water; by the touch of a neighbour's hand; by the taste of bread and wine; by the smell of 2000 candles extinguished all at once. I wanted Mennonites to experience such things.

How could our Mennonite tradition—so word heavy, so leery of the human body—dovetail with the unabashed use of light, sound, touch, taste and smell to plunge us body and spirit into Jesus' life, death and resurrection? I sensed that more embodied ways of worshipping could usher us in new ways into the watershed of God's grace and God's purposes for our world.

But translating elements from high church traditions into Mennonite worship took considerable discernment, not to mention new practical skills. During a Mennonite Easter Vigil Service one year, a banner which was supposed to unfurl gracefully at midnight narrowly missed the head of David Martin; it crashed to the floor just behind him as he was reading the Easter Gospel![64]

Fortunately Marlene Kropf came along to guide us, just when I and many others needed her. From 1983 until her recent retirement, she led our Mennonite denominations in entering into the seasons of the church year, in re-imagining the place of ritual, and in modeling the creation of worship services incorporating the senses for many occasions. Now, says Marlene, we Mennonites:[65]

> are ready to acknowledge that God works and speaks in material ways, in words, silence, relationships, symbols, mystery—in fact in any way God chooses.

The Mennonite liturgical renewal of the late 1980's and 1990's fit me, and also, I believe, deepened the spirituality of the churches I served. Creating and leading liturgies with accompanying visuals was one of my deepest joys as a pastor. Thanks be to God for such convergences!

I do wonder whether I overdid it on occasion. For when I returned to St. Jacobs to mark the 25th anniversary of my ordination, the long-time church administrator greeted me with these words: "So where's the litany? I was expecting a litany!"

---

[64] The service, held at Waterloo North that year, was one of a series planned by pastors from the K-W Ministerial of MCEC.

[65] Before her recent retirement, Marlene was a professor at AMBS and a denominational minister in the areas of worship and spiritual formation ."Q&A with Marlene Kropf," in *The Mennonite*, September 2010, (Vol. 13, No.9),15.

Dancing Chalice

In the mid-1990's I created this worship poem while on a silent retreat:

> The Creator made me
> to
> dance
> the
> new
> creation
> with
> her
>
> graceful and sturdy
> uplifted in praise
> with mind and body
> renewed
>
> open to receiving
> the reign of God
>
> and offering
> its refreshment
> in sacraments
> old and new
>
> always
> moving
> with the
> Spirit of God
>
> This is
> the sacrament of praise

Thus I gained another image of myself as a ministering person. In addition to a gardener and a midwife of the Spirit, I now also pictured myself as a dancing chalice. I modeled a small chalice out of play dough, intertwining the earth colour green with a muted pink. I displayed it prominently in my study at home. And when I verged on taking myself too seriously, I imagined my play dough object as a birdbath rather than a chalice!

The poem represented, I think, the energy and stance with which I and others set about ministering during those years. At that time, I sat on a committee charged with developing a new Minister's Manual. These words from the published manual reflected our collective excitement: [66]

> We who minister now have an opportunity to resurrect old rituals for a whole array of new situations, and to invite God's Spirit to breathe new life into them, for our time.

Invigorated by my own responsiveness to God, I offered God's refreshment in rituals the church had espoused for centuries, and also crafted new ones (or new twists on old ones) to fit particular people and situations now. As a pastor, I loved working at the intersection of worship and pastoral care, where "old rituals re-imagined" led persons and congregations into new life.

Worship Ferment

Looking back, I'm amazed at all the ferment going on in worship as the Mennonite Church (MC) and the General Conference Mennonite Church (GC) courted each other in the late 1980's and early 1990's, hoping to find enough common ground to merge.

Perhaps oddly, my recollections begin with *Confession of Faith in a Mennonite Perspective*. When a draft was released in 1992 for congregations to test, I received it as a fresh expression of our faith and practice, providing new language for preaching. I welcomed its less churchy tone, as it recast basic beliefs in words that made sense

---

[66] John Rempel, ed., *Minister's Manual* (Newton: Faith and Life Press, 1998), 180.

(I hoped) to various age groups and to people with or without a Christian memory.

Hymnal: A Worship Book arrived at the same time, expanding the musical repertoire of "hymnal churches" with songs from the global church; introducing us to the Scripture-based chants of the Taize community; offering Church of the Brethren favorites such as *My Life Flows On*; acquainting us with new composers. The arrangement of the hymnal—from Gathering in Praise through Sending—gave worship committees a template as we planned services.

The Vision, Healing and Hope statement approved in 1995 drew it all together in naming a purpose for congregations:

> God calls us to be followers of Jesus Christ,
> and by the power of the Holy Spirit,
> to grow as communities of grace, joy and peace,
> so that God's healing and hope flow through us to the world.

Looking back, I'm struck that some of the "new" practices that led us towards that vision seem so unremarkable now. Many congregations now *assume*, for instance, that of course we'd borrow a horse trough to honour a request for an indoor immersion baptism. But in the 1990's and early 2000's—open to God's Spirit—we needed to find our way.

So one year the ministry team at Waterloo North offered a Longest Night Service at the winter solstice for persons who found Christmas difficult. When the war in Afghanistan began, we offered an evening service of lament, inviting persons of all ages to light a candle. As we sat in darkness watching that table of burning tea lights, God renewed our hope.

In other ministry settings, I and others created liturgies for recognizing a divorce. We planted a tree to remember a stillborn baby. We prayerfully reclaimed the space after a visitor was raped in a public washroom in a multi-faith community centre. And at a service leading up to a congregational anniversary, we burned past grievances in a metal drum in the parking lot as we sang *Amazing Grace*.

Open to God's Spirit, we found our way.

I cherish that dancing chalice. I still display her, now sagging and dusty, on a bookshelf in my study.

The dancing chalice, the gardener and the midwife each emphasized my ministry flowing from my own connection with God. They each led me towards understanding my ministry as tending the soul of a congregation, a stance I developed in conversation with Marcus, my second spiritual director.

The dancing chalice anticipated my more fluid "flowing with the river" metaphor of ministry, inspired by walking along the Conestogo. Through that metaphor I saw myself

...basking in God's steady, sturdy love towards me
...moving with the current as it flows
...knowing where some deeper channels lie and inviting others in.

I believe the "old rituals re-imagined" of the 1990's and 2000's led people to some deeper channels of the river of life, and invited them to plunge in.

Preaching
An Intimate Act

In Marilynne Robinson's wonderful novel *Gilead,* an old Presbyterian minister reflects on all those boxes in the attic, filled with 45 years of his sermons. Rev. Ames muses, "pretty nearly my whole life's work is in those boxes, which is an amazing thing to reflect on…I'm a little afraid of them." Yet he continues:[67]

> I wrote almost all of it in the deepest hope and conviction, sifting my thoughts and choosing my words, trying to say what was true. And I'll tell you frankly, that was wonderful.

For me too as a pastor, the act of writing and preaching sermons was wonderful. At the same time it was a fierce struggle. Sometimes I had to will myself to enter that struggle.

Preaching was perhaps the hardest intellectual, emotional and spiritual work I did as a pastor. It plunged me deep into the mystery of creation. It required of me a receptive stance and an intense concentration of energy. There in the depths, my spirit listened for how God's Story addressed both the life of my congregation and the world around us.

Typically I preached twice a month. Working with a worship committee, I knew the Bible text and theme for a particular sermon

---

[67] Marilynne Robinson, *Gilead* (Toronto: HarperCollins, 2004), 18-19.

at least a month in advance. I let it roll around in my head for a while. About a week and a half before the preaching date I read the text prayerfully, then browsed in sources that came to mind.

Early in sermon week, the opening story usually presented itself. At that point I checked commentaries to see whether my emerging sense of the text was in keeping with how others saw it and if not, whether I could justify taking a variant approach.

On Thursday, I willed myself to enter the creative struggle of putting words onto the computer screen. I endeavoured to go into the pulpit with a more or less complete text, since the nuance of word and phrase matter to me. But often I didn't get to the close work until Friday afternoon and Saturday. Sometimes the ending emerged between 6 and 8 a.m. on Sunday morning, although I tried to have the sermon at a place where I could preach it by Saturday night. On sermon weekends, I always hoped no one would die or have a medical emergency until after the sermon was preached.

Sleep was part of my creative process, especially my Saturday afternoon nap. If I was still searching for the sermon conclusion on Saturday night, I trusted the sleep to bring me what I needed. I usually woke up toward morning with the ending clear.

Walking was also part of my process. I remember meeting up with another preacher while strolling through Waterloo Park one Saturday afternoon. "Are you working on your sermon too?" he asked. And indeed I was.

In the act of preaching, I felt exposed. I felt like I was up there on the high wire in the circus tent, offering my congregation a glimpse into my inner self. Barbara Brown Taylor spoke for me when she described preaching as:[68]

> a form of prayer...an act of conscious self-offering in which I stand exposed before God and my neighbor, seeking relationship with them both...My nervousness has less to do with performance anxiety than it does with standing so close

---

[68] Barbara Brown Taylor, *The Preaching Life* (Cambridge: Cowley Publications, 1993), 84-85.

to the truth of who I am before God… There is more going on here than anyone can say.

I found that I could not predict in advance when a sermon would connect with people in a powerful way. Nor could I predict when I would lose myself in the act of preaching, simply flowing with what I had been given. When these things happened, I offered profound thanks to God. When I felt like a sermon missed the mark, I left church that day with a desolate spirit.

I was always ravenously hungry at lunchtime on Sunday. Then I needed a long nap. My Sabbath time, which stretched from Sunday afternoon through Monday noon, was essential for smoothing out my spirit and renewing my energy.

A Backwards Glance

When I completed my last longer-term pastorate in 2005, I wondered: which Bible stories beckoned when I wasn't constrained by the lectionary? Which themes grounded my preaching? What did these choices reveal about me, about the congregations I served, about the era of church life during which I ministered? How did I engage—or not—the issues of the day? What is my best "voice" in preaching? And finally—how does preaching impact a congregation's spiritual development over time?

Entering the wonder and the fear, I took six months to read and reflect on my 18 years of sermons up to that time, arranged loosely by date in bulging file folders. I ingested the sermons in chronological order, took notes, created lists and charts. Somewhat unexpectedly, I found myself engaged in hard emotional and spiritual work; I had to stop at six sermons a day. When I explained to other preachers what I was doing, several responded, "Oh my, you're brave!"

Before I began, I guessed at seven recurring themes. I hoped they offered a healthy diet, including God's nourishment of us and our call to extend God's hospitality to others. I hoped I preached these themes in such a way that both old timers and newcomers could engage with them:

- *God's steadfast love, the bedrock of our faith*
- *God's holistic healing into grace, discipleship and community*
- *The church as a body and a sign*
- *Feasting at God's table*
- *Viewing our culture through the lens of the gospel*
- *Taking time for God in our culture of busyness*
- *Being open to the surprise of God's Spirit*

As I read, three other frequent offerings jumped out at me:
- *Gratitude as a countercultural expression*
- *Basic Anabaptist-Mennonite beliefs, inspired by the "new" (1995) Confession of Faith*
- *Flowing with the river of life as a congregation, living out our unique vocation.*

From time to time, Bible characters demanded to appear in person. Of course various Mary's had their say—Mary, the astonished mother of Jesus; Mary of Bethany with her expensive jar of pure nard; Mary Magdalene, the first witness to Jesus' resurrection. A disciple of Jesus named Susanna asked for time every so often.[69] And one summer Dinah the sister of Joseph unsettled us all as she told her story. After she departed I continued, "God's salvation requires that the stories of violated women like Dinah be told. The telling of the story is part of salvation."[70]

A Sacred Trust…A Force Field

In 2005 as those 18 years of sermons replayed in my head, I identified my "best preaching voice" as an evocative encouraging one that nudges people towards new life and growth. In a seminar I led for MCEC pastors that fall, I concluded:[71]

What happens when we preach to a congregation is a mystery,

---

[69] See Luke 8:3.

[70] From my sermon *"Is There Hope for This Family?"* August 30, 1992, St. Jacobs Mennonite Church. See Genesis 34 for the rape of Dinah.

[71] I shared these reflections with five ministerials in MCEC.

and needs to be. To engage in preaching is a sacred privilege and trust. We bring everything we have and are to it. It is an intimate encounter. The act of preaching is one way of tending the soul of a congregation significantly over time.

When I said that eight years ago, I wondered: am I overstating things? Does preaching *really* tend the soul of a congregation in a way that matters?

Now as I write this reflection in 2013, I'm no longer the pastor of a congregation. I do preach occasionally as a member of the preaching team at Rockway Mennonite Church, where I worship. Recently our pastor played for us preachers a video clip which makes a drastic claim. In it, Brian McLaren suggests that over time, preachers and their sermons create a force field in a congregation.

According to McLaren, we preachers are like magnets placed into a grouping of iron filings, creating a force field. Our preaching helps create a field that affects every other dimension of church life. Or, to put it another way, our preaching creates an environment in which a certain eco-system can flourish.[72]

How lovely it is to imagine that my sermons and those of my preaching colleagues over the years have been that potent! How lovely to imagine that sermons actually create an environment where sightings of God's reign can be recognized and can flourish. What a powerful way to "tend the soul of a congregation."

I'm drawn to McLaren's daring claim. Yet I also admire the perspective of the fictional Rev. Ames as he ruminates on the eventual disposal of his boxes of sermons. His wife should save a few of them, he thinks. Then the church should make a huge bonfire of the rest, with hotdogs and marshmallows—a fall festival. "They were what they were," he concludes, "and that's that."[73]

---

[72] Brian McLaren, *Preaching Moments* video clip for March 11, 2012, workingpreacher.org.
[73] *Gilead*, 245.

Baptism Sermon
You Are God's Beloved

For all whose baptisms I officiated (or intended to!)

My last few weeks as pastor at Waterloo North spun out in ways I had not expected. A nasty cold morphed into Ramsey Hunt Syndrome, a viral infection related to chicken pox, shingles and Bell's palsy. Balance issues and temporary mild facial paralysis meant that I had to miss the baptisms of two middle-aged men two weeks before my term ended. One of our lay ministers read my sermon that morning; another lay minister conducted the baptisms.

Not being able to conduct those baptisms or preach that sermon were severe disappointments for me. Here is the sermon.[74]

"You are my son, the beloved. You are my daughter, the beloved. With you I am well-pleased. I call you to a life filled with meaning and purpose."

Who wouldn't respond with joy to such words of welcome and invitation? According to the Gospel narrative, such an affirmation

---

[74] Sermon prepared by Sue C. Steiner for Waterloo North Mennonite Church, January 9, 2005. Carol Shantz read the sermon that morning; Leonard Friesen conducted the baptisms.

graced Jesus' baptism through the signs of voice and dove.

How easy it would be if the sky opened for us; if God's Spirit conveyed with a fluttering of wings in audible voice: "You are my beloved son. You are my beloved daughter. With you I am well pleased." On the other hand, if such a thing did happen for us, we'd probably not tell anyone for fear of being labeled crazy.

And yet we long for signs of God's love and acceptance, or at least I do. We long at the same time to know we are called to something. We long for our gifts to be released, so that our lives have meaning and purpose.

For most of us, God's love and God's call come mediated rather than directly—mediated through events, books, music, people, communities, lively conversation, maybe even lively conversation around the words of a confession of faith. Many times God's love and God's call slip through our pores when we're hardly paying attention; we absorb them over time rather than in an instant.

And yet for us as well as for Jesus, baptism is the symbolic event where being loved by God and being called by God come together in a profound way. In our ever-so-serious Mennonite intentionality about baptism, perhaps we're in danger of missing the sheer joy of it.

In our ever-so-serious talk of sin and accountability, perhaps we're in danger of missing those words of sheer grace: "You are my child, the beloved." In our ever-so-serious leaning into discipleship, perhaps we're in danger of missing the wonder of God's Spirit releasing our gifts.

When we submit to the waters of baptism, we receive more than a certificate and a handshake. When we submit to the waters of baptism, we agree to see our same old world with someone else's eyes and to feel its pain with someone else's heart. When we submit to the waters of baptism, we are claimed by a person and a dream. It's as if we are transported to a different world, even though we stay right here.

Now of course we often find ourselves transported to different worlds. I've been known to doze on the couch with background music playing when suddenly I hear three bars of music. I wake up. Maybe I even sit bolt upright. For those three bars of music lift me right out of my living room. Suddenly I'm on safari with Robert Redford and Meryl Streep. I'm managing a coffee plantation. I'm shooting lions. I'm lounging over dinner in a gorgeous landscape with monkeys watching the turntable of an old record player out of which come those same three bars of Mozart.

A whole new world has claimed me—the movie *Out of Africa*. Those three bars of Mozart take me there.

Now in baptism, it's God's dream that claims us, and Jesus takes us there. God's dream takes us to a landscape more gorgeous and rugged and full of contrast than the Rift Valley of Kenya or the Isle of Iona on the coast of Scotland. It's called the kingdom of God.

God's dream invites us into something more thrilling than shooting lions. It's called standing back in astonishment when lions lie down with lambs.

God's dream invites us into something more challenging than managing a coffee plantation higher than coffee has ever been grown before. It's called fitting our deepest desire to the world's deepest need.

Now to participate in God's dream we need to give up the notion that really we're each just a piece of junk. Sometimes at a low ebb in life, sometimes when we're no longer expecting it, something happens so that we are able to actually hear: "You are my son, the beloved. You are my daughter, the beloved. With you I am well pleased." When we let ourselves be reoriented to God, when we let ourselves be claimed by Jesus, we find that we are not a piece of junk. Far from it. For we carry God's image and likeness within us. We're meant to live out this identity and take up our callings in the world.

Sometimes the Spirit of Christ surprises us by saying, "Won't you trust me to take off those old dirty bandages? Let's clean out this old wound, and see if it's ready to heal." Sometimes God's Spirit surprises us by saying, "Your life is not junk, but it does need redirection." Sometimes God's Spirit surprises us with an invitation we finally can't resist: "Let's see how you and all these brothers and sisters can together embody my dream."

Oh it's true, it takes years and years to live into our baptism. Whether we're baptized at age 14 or 71 or at that point in life dubbed "middle age," it takes a lifetime. It takes a lifetime to let our identity as God's beloved child truly take hold. It takes a lifetime to explore all the nooks and crannies of God's grace. It takes a lifetime to see God's world with the eyes of Jesus the Christ, and to feel its pain with his heart. It takes a lifetime to let God's Spirit release our gifts towards God's dream.

But the One who began a good work in us will bring it to completion. May it be so for you, Ross. May it be so for you, Daniel. May it be so for all of us.

Thanks be to God!

Reflection
The Ohio at Ripley

The cover photo for this book, taken from above the town of Ripley, Ohio, leads me into realities far more complex and dynamic than its placid waters suggest.

When I'm actually *on* a river I can't see what lies beyond the next bend. I need to trust the current to carry me. But 100 steps above the Ohio at Ripley, I view the river from a kind of omniscient perspective. My eyes and my spirit take in two bends as I look downstream, and several more if I turn to face upstream. The present moment expands to include where I've come from and where I'm going, and this comforts me.

Yet the Ohio River at Ripley has a story to tell beyond flowing from its origins in Pittsburgh to the mighty Mississippi. The river at Ripley tells not only a familiar story of flowing *with* the current, but also a story of rowing *across* the current. For in the nineteenth century, it was at Ripley that nearly 2000 escaping slaves and their river guides crossed the dangerous boundary from the slave state of Kentucky to the free state of Ohio.

At the top of the hill above Ripley, just out of the photo's range, is a stop on the Underground Railroad known as Rankin House. The Rankins—Presbyterian minister John, his wife Jean and their 13 children—apparently hid most of the 2000 who crossed into freedom, expressing pride at never having "lost a passenger."

This placid photo reminds me of the courage and determination of the Rankins, the escaped slaves, and their river pilots. It reminds me that when I am a river pilot, there are options beyond "going with the flow." It reminds me that sometimes I'm called to row across the current. It reminds me that when God's Spirit invites me to lean into new life for myself and others, it may mean taking some risks. It may require of me courage sustained over a long time.

Surprised by God's Spirit
Rowing Across the Current

**In memory of Aunt Mildred and Uncle Curt
In memory of James S. Wenger**

When I was five years old, my favorite childhood cousin and best friend Helen moved away. My Uncle Curt, Aunt Mildred and three of their daughters left our traditional Mennonite community in Pennsylvania and moved 150 miles away to a place called Centereach, Long Island, New York. To me, Centereach was a mysterious place way at the other end of the world, or at least the other side of New York City.

My cousins' move introduced me to the Empire State Building, a lovely stretch of seashore, and pizza. It also plunged me at a tender age into the joy, the pain and the confusion of a major change of thinking on the part of the Mennonite Church. The Holland Tunnel enabled us Pennsylvania Mennonites to easily cross the physical boundary of the Hudson River, emerging into New York City and beyond. Crossing the boundary into a different way of thinking was much more challenging.[75]

---

[75] Situations like "The Centereach Story" also occurred in the Mennonite Conference of Ontario and other district conferences of the (Old) Mennonite Church in the 1950's.

The Centereach Story

It was 1952. World War II was over. But Mennonites in rural and small town America would never be the same. The War had ushered us into a larger world, and into new understandings of evangelism, service and peace. Discipleship based in separate communities with distinctive dress codes was beginning to give way to something else, something we could only glimpse, something which thrust us into a different sort of engagement with our world.

As part of this new vision, the Franconia Mennonite Mission Board began work in a semi-rural area of Long Island which was quickly evolving into suburbia. They invited Uncle Curt and Aunt Mildred to go to Centereach, and they went. Uncle Curt had no particular training for this new venture. He had been a "market man" by trade, working at his family's meat, poultry and egg stand at the Reading Terminal in Philadelphia, then running his own store elsewhere in the city.

In the market business, Uncle Curt met all sorts of people. He loved people, and could talk easily to anybody about anything. These natural abilities put him in good stead in Centereach. So Uncle Curt made contacts with people, Aunt Mildred fed them, and before long a group began worshipping at the Fire Hall, then in the basement of their home, with Sunday school classes in the girls' bedrooms.

Children came to Vacation Bible School, and some adults made commitments to Christ. Folks of various backgrounds worshipped together, persons began to heal from difficult life situations, and lonely people found a place to belong. Soon a small church building was constructed on the adjoining vacant lot.

As a child I read the frank letters from Aunt Mildred to my mom with much fascination. Soon it was clear, even to me, that the realities at Centereach didn't mesh very well with the dress code and certain other expectations back home.

A persistent question popped up in many forms: to become a member at Centereach, were these new Christians obliged to look like Franconia Mennonites 150 miles away? Must all jewelry be prohibited, including wedding bands? What about facial hair for men?

For some who came to faith in Centereach, the ban against weddings rings made no sense. It just didn't fit with their experience. One man tearfully told Uncle Curt that he longed to join this new church, but he had worn a wedding band for 20 years, and to take it off now would seem like an act of unfaithfulness to his wife. And at least one married couple, divorced from their previous partners, found that their desire to be members at Centereach could not be accommodated by conference regulations.

As I see it, leaders back home in Pennsylvania valued discipleship and Mennonite peoplehood very highly. In the early 1950's, a majority of them felt the need to "hold the line" in an attempt to keep a fragmenting community together. At the same time, I believe they truly wanted to extend God's hospitality in Centereach and other places. They were caught between these two impulses.

Meanwhile, Uncle Curt and Aunt Mildred laboured on at Centereach until 1964, when Curt accepted the call to pastor a church in Maryland. The Mennonite mission at Centereach closed five years later. The building was eventually used by another evangelical group; now a Buddhist temple offers spiritual sustenance on the same site.

The impulse for mission pulled the Franconia Conference in a direction it was not yet ready to go. It seems to me that the call to extend God's hospitality often does that to us. It takes us in surprising directions we can scarcely handle. It compels us to examine deeply held assumptions. It forces us to see boundaries we are erecting between ourselves and others. Often it requires nothing less than our own conversion.

Reverberations of Centereach

In both congregations I pastored longer term, my first sermon opened with "the Centereach Story," anchored in the conversions of Peter and Cornelius in Acts 10. The Peter/Cornelius story has become a major biblical touchstone for me. I experience it as an underground stream of God's love and mercy, ushering the early church and us into dimensions of God's hospitality beyond imagining.

The writer of the book of Acts pulls out all the stops. He shows us Peter, a leader of the fledgling church in Jerusalem, wrenched out of an ingrained way of thinking, doing and being. He shows us Peter completely surprised by God's Spirit. He shows us Peter led into a paradigm shift by means of trance and holy coincidence—a whole pileup of ways God was known to speak beyond reason.

The story is of such significance that the writer tells it twice, from two different angles. Everyone acts promptly, embracing a massive change without so much as blinking: what Peter always assumed to be unclean apparently isn't! God shows no partiality! Gentiles may become Christian without becoming Jewish first! How do we know? Because the Spirit comes upon Cornelius and his Gentile cohorts in the very same way the Spirit manifested herself at the Jewish Pentecost.

"Who was I that I could hinder God?" asks Peter. And according to the writer of Acts, the folks back home fall silent, then praise God.

Yet if we read the rest of the book of Acts and the letters of Paul, we find it wasn't quite that easy. It took another 50 years or so for this surprise of the Spirit to fully take hold. It took conflict between leaders and compromises that lasted for awhile and then fell apart, as the church shaped and reshaped what it could possibly mean that God shows no partiality between Jew and Gentile.

With the Peter and Cornelius story in view, I replay the sad tale of Centereach and see the obvious. The paradigm of active engagement in our world eventually overtook the previous one of preserving a bounded community with identity markers like the ban on weddings rings. But it took a nearly a generation—and a lot of pain.

It strikes me that in Mennonite congregations we've repeatedly faced Centereach-type revelations over the last decades as we've inched towards a missional church paradigm. Often our desire to extend the community is in tension with our desire to be keepers of the community we already have. We keep renegotiating whom we will receive and under what terms.

Of the hospitality challenges I have encountered as a church leader, none has been as wrenching for me as the church's struggle to acknowledge that gay and lesbian folks are already part of our congregations, and to continue extending God's hospitality and our welcome when this reality becomes known.

Jim and the Scarlatti Tape

More than 20 Decembers ago, Sam and I received a brown jiffy bag in the mail. The customs declaration said "music tape," and we saw that the sender was Jim Wenger, a Goshen College friend with whom we'd lost contact. We had recently found each other again, exchanging letters that fall.

Sam and I kept looking at that brown bag under the tree and wondering: what could this be? Why is Jim sending us a music tape after all these years? Finally on Christmas morning we found out. The tape featured an accomplished pianist playing 20 sonatas by the composer Scarlatti. The pianist was not some person unknown to us, or someone famous we'd vaguely heard about. The pianist was Jim himself, recorded by his long-time partner Peter.

Forty-five years ago, Jim had been a promising musician. And according to Goshen College lore, nobody else had ever received a grade of A+ in Mary Oyer's Introduction to Fine Arts class. But then Jim stopped playing piano, just stopped, and didn't touch it for more than 20 years.

When Jim came out as a gay person, that experience—together with being expelled from Goshen College as one of the editors of *Menno-Pause*—left him feeling rejected by the Mennonite communities which had nourished him. Somehow in this mix, Jim could no longer bring himself to play piano. That gift, an expression of Jim, lay dormant all those years.

So Jim's tape of Scarlatti sonatas was actually a coded message of sorts. Through it, Jim was saying to his family and friends, "I can express myself freely again. I have found some measure of healing. I'm offering what I have and who I am through this tape. Here it is. Here I am."

The lively music of Scarlatti fit Jim so well. It reminded me of him every time I listened to it. For in college, Jim had been a pretty wired sort of guy. He talked with his hands, which made riding in a car with him at the wheel a rather dangerous venture, especially on the narrow curvy roads of his native Lancaster County.

The next year Jim's Christmas tape featured Scott Joplin's ragtime tunes, and the year after that the music of Grieg. During his Schubert year he suffered a heart attack, then contracted a hospital superbug. He died in the same hospital where he had worked as a supply clerk since leaving Goshen in 1967, leaving behind Peter, his partner of almost 30 years.

The Body of Christ, Broken

On a personal level I owe Jim an immense debt of gratitude. At one point I attempted to romanticize our friendship, imagining that I would marry him. Jim played along for a bit, then had the honesty, courage and good sense to tell me—as well as Sam and other Goshen friends—that he was gay. Thus Jim saved me from a life I don't want to try to contemplate.

I'm sure that knowing Jim and other gay and lesbian friends has impacted my engagement with "the homosexuality issue" beyond measure. It ensured that when I became a pastor, I would approach hospitality to persons with same-gender attraction from my gut. I didn't want anyone else's encounter with the church to silence their piano playing for 20 years!

The experience of Jim and others whispered wisdom to me as I engaged with gay and lesbian congregants or their families, and as I participated in various study and discernment processes over the years. Having LGBT[76] friends helped me resist at least to some degree the common wisdom in decision making circles that "keeping the church together" is the primary agenda. Over the years I came to the conviction that our exclusion of LGBT folks from full participation was in fact *not* "keeping the church together," but rather severing limbs in a manner painful for all concerned.

In 2006, I had the holy privilege of bringing greetings from the General Board of Mennonite Church Canada[77] to the Open Spirit conference in Toronto, sponsored by the Brethren Mennonite Council for Lesbian, Gay, Bisexual and Transgender Interests and a comparable Lutheran group. I began by saying:[78]

> I'm happy to be here this morning, to bring greetings...Yet I'm also sad to be here. I'm sad whenever the Body of Christ is broken, and clearly in 2006 in North America, the Body of Christ is broken over different practices and perspectives around the participation of gay and lesbian persons in the church.

I described the national church's stated desire to move toward difficult conversations rather than moving away from them. Then I closed with my own passionate hope:

> I look forward to the day when the Body of Christ is not broken. I don't know what that day will look like or how we'll get there. I do believe that God's Spirit is active. I believe God's Spirit can and does move in all parts of the painfully broken Body of Christ.

---

[76] Lesbian Gay Bi-sexual and Transgendered
[77] I served on the General Board as chair of the Christian Formation Council.
[78] Sue C. Steiner, "Greetings from the General Board of Mennonite Church Canada" to the Open Spirit Conference, Toronto, Ontario, July 29, 2006.

In the fall of 2012 I participated in a communion service at a Presbyterian church in the United States. I doubt that I will ever forget it.

The communion was the culmination of the marriage celebration of our friends Carol and Katie, long-time active members of that congregation. In her homily, the resident pastor spoke passionately of Jesus' table hospitality. Then Katie and Carol repeated the same vows they had pledged to each other 28 years earlier in a private gathering at their rural property. After the vows, the seven pastors in attendance and the couple themselves served communion to all who wished to partake.

In that communion service I caught a glimpse of the dismembered body of Christ being sewn back together—heart by heart, limb by limb, one act of gospel hospitality at a time.

Navigating
Uncharted Waters

Roaring Waters
Grief, Longing and Delicate New Life

One afternoon in June 2007 I reveled in exploring the Tel Dan Nature Reserve on the Golan Heights. Sam and I had just begun a two-week sojourn in Israel, Jordan and the Palestinian Territories with friends well-acquainted with the region.

Setting out from Tiberias, I loved driving along the Sea of Galilee, stopping at churches commemorating the Beatitudes or Simon Peter or the feeding of the multitudes. Natural beauty, religious history and current political realities intertwined to make our trek north to Tel Dan and nearby Hermon Stream stand out in memory.

I marveled at the wide, well-lit, well-maintained highway as we headed into the sparsely-inhabited northern reaches of currently-held Israeli territory. Finally the obvious struck me—this road wasn't built for the benefit of kibbutz dwellers or tourists but rather as an access route for military troops and equipment. At one place the highway looked like a landing strip—and probably was.

An almost mystical sense came over me as we drove through remote hilly terrain. Since I was working through a major transition that spring, my receptors were likely more attuned than usual. I had ended my last long-term pastorate two years earlier, and was now completing my last stint of interim ministry. At age 60 I was moving into a ministry focus of coaching pastors and offering spiritual direction. While I felt drawn to this focus and believed it was of God, my anticipation mingled with feelings of grief and loss.

Thus I explored the Tel Dan and Hermon Stream nature parks that day with my physical senses and my spiritual sensibilities heightened. The beauty of the landscape in sight of Mount Hermon drew me in. So did the excavations of the Canaanite cultic center of Dan, where ancient Israel's King Jeroboam erected a golden calf in the 9th century BCE. Today's political realities intruded as I took in the panoramic view from a 1967 Israeli command post. My eyes and my spirit saw not only the slopes of Mount Hermon, but also an abandoned former Syrian outpost and a Lebanese village.

Never were my senses so keenly attuned as on a nature walk through a lush wooded area dubbed "the garden of Eden." The earth felt spongy underfoot. Water surrounded me—seeping out of the ground, cascading down rocks and flowing across our path in rivulets almost too wide to jump over. We could scarcely hear each other over the roar of converging waters as they formed themselves into a fast-moving stream.

I was standing on the spot where the Dan River begins, created by rain and snowmelt passing through the rock of Mt. Hermon and emerging in a myriad of springs at its foot. Water seeping from other nearby springs converged into other fast-moving streams. Together the Dan and neighbouring streams formed the headwaters of the Jordan River, its contested waters so essential for a thirsty land.

That day in 2007 my spirit felt inundated by all this seeping, cascading, roaring, path-flooding water. Then it dawned on me that these rushing headwaters of the Jordan were an integral part of a 2500-year-old lament to which I often turned. Psalm 42-43 ministered to me that summer as I came to terms with leaving congregational ministry.

I knew that part of my grief focused on no longer presiding over the worship life of a congregation, one of my greatest joys in ministry. I'd grasped that the grief of the ancient song writer had a similar source:

> These things I remember,
> > as I pour out my soul:
> how I went with the throng,
> > and led them in procession to the house of God,
> with glad shouts and songs of thanksgiving,
> > a multitude keeping festival. (Ps. 42:4, NRSV)

What I'd missed is that the Psalm writer, likely a temple singer or worship leader, composed his lament in a place of geographic and spiritual exile in the northern reaches of Israel in sight of Mt. Hermon—the very locale I explored on that afternoon spent at Tel Dan and Hermon Stream.

> My soul is cast down within me;
> > therefore I remember you from the land of Jordan
> > > and of Hermon, from Mt. Mizar.
> Deep calls to deep at the thunder of your cataracts;
> > all your waves and your billows have gone over me.
> > > (Ps. 42: 6-7, NRSV)

Suddenly I realized: he's talking about the headwaters of the Jordan! In sight of Mt. Hermon he too hears the thunder of the cataracts; he too feels inundated by "your waves and billows going over me." In exile from Jerusalem, in Israel's far north, the rushing waters help him sing his homesickness for "God's house"—for his usual place of worship and service where God's presence is made known.

Three times the Psalm-writer combines loss and hope with this refrain:

> Why are you cast down, O my soul?
> > and why are you disquieted within me?
> Hope in God; for I shall again praise him,
> > my help and my God.

I prayed these words from time to time over the next year.

Slowly the memory of "leading the throng in worship" took on the sepia tone of a cherished old photograph; gratitude emerged, with just a tinge of longing. Gradually I realized: of course I can praise God as a "regular" member of a congregation!

I do continue to look at worship with a certain eye—just as a retired architect looks at building design with a certain eye or a retired feed mill owner looks at a field of barley with a certain eye. But now as I drink in the worship life of the congregation I attend or worship with other churches on occasion, I no longer feel exiled. I feel at home.

It strikes me that those seeping, noisy headwaters of the Jordan signify a place of creation and creativity as well as of loss and longing. At Tel Dan, amidst much commotion, living streams converge to give drink to a thirsty land, as they have for millennia. And my own places of grief host delicate new life for myself and for others.

Nurse Logs: Hosting Delicate New Life

Already when I left my first congregation, an image combining loss and new life arrived to sustain me. When I resigned as a pastor at St. Jacobs after nearly nine years I wondered: who will I be for this corporate body after I'm physically gone from the scene? I knew my resignation meant giving up many relationships in which I'd shared sacred moments with people. Yet I thought: perhaps I'm still "there" with them in some very different sense. But I couldn't quite imagine how.

Then that summer, Sam and I explored the Olympic Rain Forest on the coast of Washington State, one of the only temperate rain forests in the United States. We walked past many fallen logs lying on the forest floor. What surprised me was the beautiful variety of plant life they hosted. All sorts of new life quietly burst forth, lapping up nutrients as those logs decomposed. I saw a wonderful display of moss, vines, ferns, little white flowers, tree seedlings—all of them nourished by those fallen logs.

I read somewhere that such logs are called "nurse logs." And I thought—maybe that's it—maybe I'll be a nurse log for St. Jacobs Church. Maybe my ministry will now nourish them in a different way. Maybe delicate new life of all sorts will spring up there, in shapes and forms I couldn't have predicted. That thought gave me comfort. So each time I've made such a transition, I've pulled out Sam's photo of that Olympic Rain Forest nurse log and displayed it prominently in my study.

It's a great gift to me to occasionally catch glimpses of what's developing in congregations I've served. I hope for both continuity and change. If I join the congregation for a special worship service, I like to say to myself, "Oh good! There are people here I know as well as folks I don't know." I'm relieved when I discover that the next group of leaders found their way through a dilemma left over from my time.

Of course I'm gratified to see initiatives blossoming from seeds planted during my time. But I also enjoy being surprised by new directions in worship, spiritual formation or mission which I know could not have flowered under my ongoing leadership. I love to imagine myself as that nurse log.

The River Journey Continues

"God's call on our lives does NOT end at retirement," the speaker asserted forcefully. The words lodged somewhere deep within me, offering assurance. I was only 50 years old when I heard them, but I was already starting to wonder: after congregational ministry, what?

During that decade, "tending the soul of the church" became my ministry stance. Certainly it fit the way I approached pastoral ministry. It also fit my other ministries, such as offering spiritual direction, teaching pastors-in-training, and chairing the Christian Formation Council of Mennonite Church Canada. I understood all these as manifestations of "tending the soul of the church."

At age 60 it seemed natural to conclude pastoral ministry and focus on these other expressions of my call. I imagined that when I hit the magic age of 65, I would continue with more of the same at a slower pace, focusing on soul tending within our denomination. And that has indeed happened.

But gradually—somewhat to my surprise—I found myself also drawn to a different landscape. Put another way, I started looking for signs of the Spirit at work not only on the part of the river I knew, but also in other parts of the watershed. As I did so, a new metaphor emerged to express part of my calling as a "young senior."

I began to imagine myself *rehearsing the reign of God* along with others.

Rehearsing the Reign of God
I'm intrigued by the notion of *rehearsing the reign of God*. I borrowed this phrase from Diana Butler Bass, who imagines church as a sacred community where we "learn the script of God's story" and "rehearse the reign of God."[79]

The language of *rehearsal* recognizes that the reign of God is far from fully realized in our world and sometimes appears downright absent. But it seems to me that by consciously *rehearsing* the reign of God, we're putting our longing for it into action.

Perhaps this idea appeals to me because it translates the separatist model of church and world of my childhood into something much more lively, participatory, invitational and dynamic. It acknowledges that the reign of God in all its fullness is not something we humans can bring into being. But with practice we can catch enough of its spirit to notice where it's starting to happen and rehearse it together with others. And who knows—our persistent rehearsal, our persistent practice, our persistent enactment of God's reign just may help God bring it to pass. Here's one sample:

Each Thursday afternoon I step over a threshold into a vibrant rehearsal hall of the reign of God. Anyone who wishes is welcome to show up for the rehearsal that goes on day after day at the Waterloo Generations Thrift Shop.

The action begins as many people drop off clothes or household goods or books or furniture at the outdoor receiving area off the small parking lot. Then many volunteers take up their parts, each as he or she is able. In the crowded pricing room, a retired university librarian rubs shoulders with a home schooled child or an adult on a disability pension or the former owner of a house wares shop or a student doing community service hours. The efforts of all are

---

[79] Diana Butler Bass, *Christianity after Religion: The End of Church and the Birth of a New Spiritual Awakening* (New York: Harper One, 2012), 261.

gratefully incorporated.

On the sales floor, volunteers shelving goods or running the cash register mingle with a great variety of customers as the main event gets underway. When I'm on cash, I'm likely to encounter in quick succession a child overjoyed with a 50-cent stuffed toy, a dad who can't afford to take home a $5 pair of skates that might not fit his son, a student furnishing an apartment, an antique lover paying $200 for an item in the silent auction, and a woman who has learned to dress smartly in clothes someone else discarded.

As we enact this parable of recycling and reusing six days a week, we support the work of Mennonite Central Committee around the world. Some days I shake my head and think: this largely volunteer-run model is pretty messy and really shouldn't work—but it does. Volunteering weekly at the thrift shop has become one of my ways of rehearsing the reign of God together with others.[80]

The church of Jesus Christ will always be a primary spiritual home where I first look for the script and for people to rehearse it with me. But I will look elsewhere also, knowing that God's reign extends way beyond the church and that the church is not always at the forefront of understanding and living into the script.

I expect my calling in this stage of life will take me deeper into my local community—whether that means volunteering at the thrift shop or offering a book club at the local women's prison or sitting on the spiritual resources council of a social service agency. I imagine myself stepping out of the river craft I know onto various shores. I hope my ability to notice what the Spirit is doing in other parts of the watershed will deepen, enriching the soul care I continue to offer.

An Age of the Spirit

Various Christian writers believe we are now entering *an age of the Spirit.* Some speak of this modestly, likening it to other periodic

---

[80] In the fall of 2013 the new Thrift on Kent will open, incorporating Waterloo Generations and another MCC thrift shop. The rehearsal will continue there.

awakenings such as the one which enlivened my grandmother 112 years ago. Others such as Phyllis Tickle see something far grander, more like a giant church rummage sale occurring every 500 years or so. After each such rummage sale, says Tickle, some radically new forms of church emerge, while at the same time the old form of church is refurbished.[81]

It's commonplace these days to suggest that the church is now navigating through uncharted waters, as various old assumptions and forms of church life die and the shape of the future cannot yet be seen. Many speak of the need for adaptive change. I believe we are indeed navigating uncharted waters. I believe we need to be very attuned to the Spirit.

I see in many pastors today an attitude that cheers me. I see in them an absence of handwringing as we face into the future. Instead I catch from them an excitement about being the church in this era which reminds me of myself 25 years ago. I rejoice when I observe them waiting on God's Spirit, flowing with the river in trust. I'm hopeful when they invite us to look for the Spirit's work in parts of the watershed we have not traditionally explored.

As for me, I'm no longer that chalice offering God's refreshment to a particular community of faith. I do have an inkling of where some of the deeper channels of the river lie, and I want to keep inviting others in.

Most importantly, I want to keep moving with the current of God's grace and intent for our world, wherever it flows. I want the river to carry me. I want to be curious and unafraid, open to surprise about the river up ahead and the landscape to be explored around the next bend.

A hymn I've loved since I first sang it 21 years ago keeps luring me down the river, animating my journey. It begins like this:[82]

---

[81] Phyllis Tickle, *The Great Emergence* (Grand Rapids: Baker Books, 2008), 14-15.
[82] Robert Lowry, "My life flows on" in *Hymnal: A Worship Book* (Scottdale: Mennonite Publishing House, 1992), 580.

> My life flows on in endless song,
> above earth's lamentation.
> I catch the sweet, though far off hymn
> that hails a new creation.
> No storm can shake my inmost calm
> while to that Rock I'm clinging.
> Since love is Lord of heav'n and earth,
> how can I keep from singing?

As is usually the case with me and 19th century hymn texts, sometimes I'm content to sing it as is, but at other times I want to nuance it. Some days I'm fine with imagining the song of new creation "far off," located "above" earth's lamentation. Other days, I'd prefer to sing it like this:

> My life flows on in endless song;
> *amidst* earth's lamentation
> I catch *those clear, surprising tones*
> that *hail* a new creation.
> No storm can shake my inmost calm
> while to that Rock I'm clinging.
> Since love is Lord of heav'n and earth,
> how can I keep from singing?

The Duck Pond (Clair Creek), Waterloo, Ontario—Viewed from the snowy bank

Afterword
Meditation by a Kentucky Pond

Recently I spent a retreat day at the mother house of the Sisters of Loretto in rural Kentucky.[83] The retreat leader invited us to go outside for half an hour, look around in silence, see what attracted our notice, and simply pay attention to it.

I heard a faint rustle as I headed for a small pond I'd glimpsed earlier. I walked around the pond, then stepped back, climbed a small hill, and observed the scene from that perspective.

From up above I saw such a simple thing. In the breeze, the current in the pond flowed in the gentlest of waves, all—of course—headed the same direction. Every branch of every tree and every stalk of ornamental grass also bent gently in the same direction.

No branch appeared in danger of snapping off. No stalk of ornamental grass looked like it would break. Every branch, every stalk, every wave appeared willing to let the breeze have its way, seemingly without resistance. It looked so gentle, so graceful, and I loved the soft rustle.

And I wondered: is this how the Spirit wants to nudge me? If so, why am I so afraid of bending?

---

[83] The Sisters of Loretto began as a teaching order on the Kentucky frontier in 1824. In the last 50 years, they've become known in North America for their peace, justice and environmental witness. Their Kentucky site is now a retirement community for the order, peopled by still-feisty nuns, as well as a retreat centre.

I wondered: is this how the Spirit wants to move us as a church—gracefully, all in the same direction?

Is this graceful picture what it looks like to God when together we respond to the Spirit's leading?

Now really, there's nothing remarkable about what I observed in that faint rustle by the pond while on retreat in Kentucky. I could see exactly the same things on my daily walk around the duck pond in Waterloo. God may be eager to show me such things frequently. But often I'm too preoccupied, too full of internal noise, too distracted to pay attention, even on my morning walk.

After all, we live in a noisy culture, with many voices calling out to us, promising security or excitement if only we'd consume the products and experiences they have on offer. Sometimes it's hard to distinguish God's voice in all that clamour.

So I wonder: in North America in 2013, how does God try to attract our attention as individuals, as congregations, as Christian people?

Sometimes in history God has used noisy ways, powerful ways, symbolized by the fierce wind, earthquake and fire that accompanied the revelation to Moses on Mt. Sinai. At other times, God has used quiet ways, the still small voice—silence even—to announce God's purpose and presence, as with Elijah on the same Mt. Sinai.

So I wonder: in North America in 2013, by what means do you and I expect God to speak—if we expect God to speak at all? Are we more receptive to God showing up in signs and wonders? Or in gentle whispers emerging out of silence?

I wonder whether in North America in 2013, God might be inviting us to listen to the quiet. I wonder if we need silence to hear the Spirit interceding for us with sighs too deep for words. I wonder if we can better receive the peace and the challenge God offers if they come in whispers rather than thunderclaps.

I wonder if God stands ready to approach us often with simple metaphors of trees and waves all gently leaning in the Spirit's direction. I wonder.

Gratitudes

As I release this book, I am grateful:

- For all who blessed me, knowingly or not, during my formative years in Souderton, my college days in Goshen, and the years when my call to church ministries took root in Ontario. Some are named at the beginning of essays; others are embedded within essays; others are part of groups named.

- For my ministry colleagues these past 25 years, mostly unnamed. Special thanks to the prayer group, whose members listened respectfully and prayed for me as this book took hold in my heart and emerged on paper.

- For persons in the congregations I've served; for pastors I've coached or taught; for my directees past and present—we've listened together for God's way for each of us and for the church in this era.

- For Scott Brubaker-Zehr and Rockway Mennonite Church—a spiritual home before and after my time "away" in pastoral ministry.

- For my manuscript readers, who offered such good counsel—Brice Balmer, Ruth Boehm, Miriam Maust, Mary Schiedel, Ellen Shenk.

- For the editorial counsel of Susan Fish (susan@storywell.ca); for the design and printing assistance of Christian Snyder at Pandora Print Shop.

- For Maggie the cat, snoozing beside me in the recycling box as I worked.

- For Sam, with whom I've shared the journey these 44 years. Often I've implored him to take a photo of yet another body of water, and usually he's obliged. His photography enriches this book, as he enriches my life. I dedicate *Flowing with the River* to him, in gratitude for his ongoing love and support.

About the Author

Sue Clemmer Steiner grew up on West Chestnut Street in Souderton, Pennsylvania, nourished by her extended family and by the neighbourhood, including Souderton Mennonite Church at the end of the block.

She graduated from Christopher Dock Mennonite High School in 1965, then ventured out to Indiana to attend Goshen College. At Goshen she edited the student newspaper, met Sam Steiner, and studied hard, graduating with a BA in English in 1969.

Sue followed Sam (by then a draft resister) to Ontario, marrying him on the lawn of Conrad Grebel College on August 2, 1969. She worked for the church-owned Provident Bookstores for 10 years, buying books for the Kitchener and London, Ontario stores. In 1973, she and Sam joined Rockway Mennonite Church in Kitchener.

Her experiences at Provident Bookstores and Rockway Church, as well as various writing assignments, led Sue to consider "church work" as a vocation. She attended Waterloo Lutheran Seminary for two years, transferring credits to what is now Anabaptist Mennonite

Biblical Seminary (AMBS) in Indiana, where she graduated with an MDiv in 1982. She served as youth minister for Mennonite Conference of Ontario and Quebec, resigning in l985 to be open to a call from a congregation.

St. Jacobs Mennonite Church called Sue as associate pastor in l987, where she was ordained on Pentecost Sunday. She ministered there through 1995, the last four years as co-pastor. After leaving St. Jacobs, Sue took training in offering spiritual direction from Shalem Institute and AMBS, and served as an interim pastor of two churches. In 1998 she accepted a call to be lead minister of Waterloo North Mennonite Church, where she served until 2005.

Sue took two more assignments as an interim pastor, then concentrated on coaching pastors, offering spiritual direction and related specialized ministries until her retirement in summer 2012. Her church committee work over the years has included chairing the Mission and Service Commission of MCEC and the Christian Formation Council of Mennonite Church Canada. She has written Sunday school curriculum for youth and adults, as well as a book on peace theology for youth called *Joining the Army that Sheds No Blood* (Herald Press, 1982).

Sue lives in Waterloo with Sam, retired librarian and archivist of Conrad Grebel University College, and with Maggie the cat. She continues to offer spiritual direction to church leaders, and enjoys volunteering in the community, for MCEC, and at Rockway Church, where she and Sam are once again active members. She looks for sightings of God's reign everywhere.